WORKING WITH
SPIRIT GUIDES

WORKING WITH
SPIRIT GUIDES

Ruth White

PIATKUS

Visit the Piatkus website!

Piatkus publishes a wide range of bestselling fiction and non-fiction, including books on health, mind, body & spirit, sex, self-help, cookery, biography and the paranormal.

If you want to:
- read descriptions of our popular titles
- buy our books over the internet
- take advantage of our special offers
- enter our monthly competition
- learn more about your favourite Piatkus authors

VISIT OUR WEBSITE AT: www.piatkus.co.uk

Copyright © 2004 by Ruth White

First published in Great Britain in 2004 by
Piatkus Books Ltd
5 Windmill Street, London W1T 2JA
email: info@piatkus.co.uk

Reprinted 2004 (twice), 2005 (twice)

The moral right of the author has been asserted

A catalogue record for this book is available
from the British Library

ISBN 0 7499 2499 3

Text design by Briony Chappell
Edited by Jan Cutler
Illustrations by Rodney Paull

This book has been printed on paper manufactured
with respect for the environment using wood from
managed sustainable resources

Typeset by Action Publishing Technology Limited, Gloucester
Printed and bound in Great Britain by
Antony Rowe Ltd, Chippenham, Wiltshire

CONTENTS

ACKNOWLEDGEMENTS

I want to thank, once again, the groups and individuals who allow me to teach, lead or help them. They ask the right questions at the right time and give the support that enables the work to unfold.

I should also like to thank Gildas, my discarnate Guide and teacher, for his presence and wisdom.

Names and identifying details in the case studies have been changed, but thanks go to those who have been so generous in giving permission for their life experiences to be used in my writing.

My publishers also deserve thanks for their vision in producing the book and their unfailing support during the writing process.

My Jack Russell, Jackson, is still with me. He is now 11 years old, but sits on my feet whilst I write. He attends almost all workshops, where he can be something of a trickster, although he never interrupts Gildas, and serves to remind everyone to stay grounded even whilst they are reaching for spiritual heights.

Ruth White can be contacted on 01273 584060.

You can also visit her website which gives details of current events and workshops: www.ruthwhite-gildas.co.uk.

For Jean,
who welcomed me to the Sussex cliffs, where I now live, and who
has since become like a sister.
With love and thanks.

INTRODUCTION

It is natural to wonder about the background of the writer of any book, to want to know the purposes that lie behind the writing of the book and where the writer is coming from. I feel that it is essential to summarise some of my own experience, especially for a book such as this, because it is on this that the book is based.

In some senses my life has been extraordinary. For as long as I can remember, I have been aware that there was another presence with me. As a child as young as three years old I sensed a tall, white, shining being that I felt must be an angel. I 'labelled' the being thus because of things I had heard discussed around me and prayers I had been taught to say. For various reasons I did not find family life easy and never felt truly bonded to my parents. Having what I thought of as my angel as friend, as confidant and protector helped me through some difficult years.

I saw angels or shining figures accompanying most adults and children. I also perceived colours around people, which changed when they were ill, angry or in emotional states. I saw fairies, nature spirits and brightly coloured energies around plants and animals, and I assumed that everyone else could see what I saw. As I gradually learned that others did not see these things or try to communicate with their otherworldly companions and helpers, I found it very strange. When I discovered that talking about what I saw made my parents angry, afraid and punishing, I learned to block out most of this vision and to keep the rest secret. Repressing and hiding my natural experience of other worlds and trying to be the sort of child my parents wanted me to be took a tremendous toll. It was not until I was 14 that it was discovered that, from birth, as far as outer vision was concerned, I had actually been able to see very little with my right eye. As my left eye seemed to be getting more and more short-sighted there were fears that I might go blind, or at best be classified as partially sighted.

My passion at school was for languages but it was decided that a university education was out of the question because it would involve too much reading and close work. I was advised to work with plants, but although I loved plants of every kind, I knew that work in a plant nursery or as a gardener could never become a fully satisfying career for me. I was then advised to take the (as then) two-year training course for teachers at a teacher training college and to specialise in teaching infants. It has long puzzled me why someone threatened with near blindness, with little interest in teaching or in young children, should have been given such advice, but I had long known that if my parents were adamant there was little point in arguing, so, in September 1956, off to the City of Leicester Teacher Training College I went.

At college my inner turmoil and my basic lack of motivation for teaching became more obvious. I was full of fears that I hardly dared express. However, my inner world was active and the shining being alongside me was very present. This being had always helped, supported and comforted me, but, knowing well by now that my experience of him was not one that others shared, I feared I was going mad.

I have found that sometimes in life, when I seem to be between a rock and a hard place and not where I would want to be by conscious choice, there is a synchronicity or serendipity that suddenly shines through and makes it obvious that I am in the right place at the right time after all. By a series of enormous coincidences I was training to teach at the only college in the country at that time which offered access to a student counselling service and so I came to meet Dr Mary Swainson. As well as being a pioneer of student counselling, Mary Swainson was a Jungian psychotherapist and also an inner brother of the spiritual and esoteric order known as the White Eagle Lodge. Of course, I did not know this latter fact during the first phase of my counselling and therapy with Mary, but something in me recognised that I had, at last, found an ally in life, to whom, without fear, I could tell all my difficulties and with whom, especially, I could share my experience of my shining friend and my fears of madness.

My childhood had been difficult and painful in many ways and I certainly needed some basic psychotherapy. But, as time went on, Mary and I talked more and more about the core experience of my life – my shining friend – and other extrasensory perceptions that I was experiencing. She encouraged me to speak to the shining presence and to ask for a name. The replies came fluently, like a sort of dictation that I perceived clearly in my head. I wrote the words down quite quickly as I received them, without taking in their full meaning until I read them or they were read back to me later. (This was not the phenomenon of automatic writing where people have been known to experience the pen and their hand moving as though driven by some other force.) It was as though someone else was standing beside me telling me word for word, but fluently, what to write.

The communicating being, whom I had known for as long as I could remember, now told us that he wished to be called Gildas – a French name, meaning, 'a messenger of truth'. He told us that he had last incarnated as a Benedictine monk in the fourteenth century in France and that now he was able to choose whether to reincarnate or not. Gildas told us then, as he continues to tell us now, that he is currently working with a large group of similar beings or Spirit Guides, on the 'other side', endeavouring to establish a link to those of us in incarnation so that teachings about the wider spiritual dimension of experience can be given and we can be helped to a clearer or broader perspective of life on earth and the problems and dilemmas we encounter.

The whole field of mediumship or channelling, as well as concepts such as reincarnation and many lifetimes, were completely new to me. I had been brought up to attend the Congregational Church, been a Sunday school teacher and had enjoyed singing in the church choir. I had tried, unsuccessfully, to fit my experience of Gildas into the church framework, but now it seemed quite natural that he should communicate fluently through me and teach me a wider frame of reference for other worlds, other states and the beings that live beyond our present dimension. My extreme confusion gradually cleared and I felt blessed and gifted instead of muddled and possibly mad.

Gildas readily answered the questions that Mary and I put to him. He explained, quite early on, that he was a Guide, not an angel. Guides are part of the human stream of consciousness and have usually incarnated on earth many times and may or may not do so again. Angels are from a different stream of consciousness, have never incarnated and never will. They are manifestations of Divine energies and they help and protect us in many different ways. Although it may be a pleasant vision to think of ourselves becoming angels when we die, apparently we do not; although, when in the other realms or worlds, we do have a lot of contact with angelic beings. Guides and angels work in harmony together but are of a different substance. In incarnation we all have a guardian angel and at least one Guide, who are particularly interested in, and supportive of, our welfare and life pathway.

On being told that Gildas had been a monk in his last incarnation, I realised that what I had previously thought was an angelic 'gown' was actually a white monk's robe, but over the years I have lost the need to see him in quite such a personified way. Now I sense him more as energy, seeing his colours and smelling his special fragrance. It only takes a few moments to make the slight shift of consciousness that enables me to receive his communications. I no longer write his words by hand, but speak them into a tape recorder or type them into my computer.

I gradually came to accept that before incarnating this time around, I made a soul contract agreement with Gildas, to learn to be a channel for his work. It is now over 46 years since my serious channelling of Gildas began, and the work has become a joint work. My life and training have given me skills in working with people and running workshops. Gildas provides the extra dimension of information. We are a team that works with great harmony and mutual respect. He is always near me, just as he was when I was a child.

Mary's help and support enabled me to live a normal life alongside my more unusual experiences. I successfully completed my teacher training, taught young children for over twenty years during which time I married, had a daughter and became a single parent when my marriage did not work out.

I had never really wanted to teach but managed to make a reasonable success of it as a career. Teaching in the local village school also made bringing up a child alone less complex.

Continuing to develop my work with Gildas and single parenthood was another matter, however. Teaching never truly made my heart sing, and as soon as I could see the way to doing so, I retrained as a psychological counsellor and psychotherapist. Becoming self-employed, as a result of this retraining, enabled me to develop my workshop programmes and spiritual consultancy work with Gildas.

What I have to say in this book is informed by my experience with Gildas and his teachings. It also combines a rich input from my psychological and psychotherapeutic interest and training and from my work as channel, writer, spiritual teacher and consultant, and healer and trainer of healers and channellers. Many co-travellers have generously shared with me their own experience of similar encounters and of those worlds that are completely different and much more subtle than our present world, but which have, nevertheless, their own rich reality, which so rewards exploration.

I want to emphasise that mainly I *can* only share my experience as it has happened and as it has been interpreted by me. Over the years I have discovered that many people have had similar experiences to mine or feel that they want to develop contacts and connections with other worlds and particularly with their Spirit Guides. Each experience is different, and yet it carries similarities. Sharing what has been learned is of mutual benefit. I have made the world of guidance my speciality and been privileged to witness the joys and sense of greater meaning and purpose in life that contact with subtle interpenetrating worlds and beings from other dimensions can bring to individuals and groups.

In present times we often say that because of the speed of modern communications the earth has seemed to contract. Perhaps this is one of the reasons why an increasing number of people also seek the sense of expansion that contact with other worlds or dimensions can bring. Modern life is also extremely demanding. We have an overload of information and weaving our way through it is not easy. Spirit Guides have an overview and help us to find a context and pattern in what is presented to us by life and the way in which it happens. They give us more information and bring hope. They tell us how we can help humanity to reach a high level of potential. They enable and encourage us to build a network of light that will help the heart of humanity to open without fear.

My vision for this book is that it will help the many people who are now beginning to explore wider spiritual dimensions in their lives. It is for those who have ever wondered about the meaning of life itself, why we are here, why certain things happen to us and the basis on which to make spiritually responsible decisions about our life paths. It is for those who have ever felt a sense of 'otherworldly' accompaniment in their lives and want to be more consciously aware of this. It is for those who long for a loving and inspiring guidance contact such as I enjoy with Gildas, whether they have already begun that search or are completely new to it. It is for those who have an instinctual faith, and a radical trust, in the spiritual future of humanity. Many such people feel themselves drawn to being a part of that group who work for contact between the different worlds and planes in order to effect a wider understanding of the greater pattern of things. It is for spiritual bridge builders.

Within the pages of this book you will find information about Spirit Guides and their teachings. There are comments on questions commonly asked about Guides and guidance. There are exercises to help you to develop your own personal connection with a Spirit Guide. These can be used whether you are a complete beginner or already have more knowledge or experience of guidance. There is information about inner worlds, chakras, subtle bodies and subtle planes to enable you to develop your energy field in order to explore other dimensions with confidence and safety. A glossary appears at the end of the book so that you can find out more about the different terms you encounter as you work through.

It is a good idea to read through the whole book and all the exercises before you begin consistently preparing to work with your Spirit Guide. After that, read each chapter in more depth and try each of the exercises in sequence from exercise 1 to exercise 11. This first use of the exercises may already lead you to your Spirit Guide if you have not already made their acquaintance, but it will certainly give you a basis on which, and from which, to select and develop your own programme for strengthening your work with Spirit Guides. It is wonderful work and I wish you much joy in it.

Chapter 1, which follows next, surveys and discusses the human quest for guidance and tells the story of two clients who were searching for the spiritual perspective on their life dilemmas.

I

The Human Quest for Guidance

This chapter looks at our need for guidance and the eternal human quandary of choice. It explores the part that religion, philosophy and psychology have to play in enabling our search for meaning, and discusses the phenomenon of mediumship, channelling and contact with Spirit Guides. The chapter ends with the stories of Karen and Anthony who sought guidance and perspective for their human dilemmas.

The eternal quandary of choice

From my psychotherapy practice alone, I know that one of the most stressful things in human life can be the dilemma of choice. We worry about making right or wrong choices, whether they are choices we still have to make or choices we made in the past. We need to 'get it right' both for ourselves and for those we love. We look back over our lives and say: 'If I had made a different choice *then* I would not be in my present dilemma *now.* I don't want to make a mistake this time' or 'Did I miss an opportunity when I decided against that job offer abroad? What might my life be like now, if I had chosen differently?'

This worry, longing, puzzlement and questioning about the crossroads we meet in life is part of our dilemma as well as part of our integrity as human beings. Most of us want a better world, a more satisfactory experience of life and a framework against which we can assess the potential or quality of our choices. We seek help, guidance and support. We often wish we could 'just be told what to do and how and when to do it' so that life could be simpler and we could concentrate on the task in hand with a sense of certainty and security.

We are great seekers of advice from experts. We need political, economic, educational, religious and social leadership. When we have big choices (or even smaller ones) to make, we turn to partners, friends, advisers, teachers and perhaps counselling or psychological self-understanding. If we hesitate overmuch in making our choices, we fear that opportunities may pass us by or be closed to us. If we fail to pass a certain exam or interview or fail to reach a desired goal, we experience a sense of rejection and may feel unworthy or depressed.

We need a framework, basis or belief system from which to make choices. We may often speak of 'bettering ourselves' or of wanting to enable the 'highest good'. We may torment ourselves about what effect *our* particular choices might have on other people. As we look at the pattern of our lives we may wonder about how far we are the victims of circumstance, how much we are subject to choices that have already been made for us at a higher level, or how to take appropriate responsibility for ourselves and others.

Predestination or free will?

Most of us, at some time in our lives, reflect on ideas about destiny and free will. We ask ourselves questions such as: 'Am I truly a self-determining being with complete freedom of choice or am I on a predestined path and thus, in real life terms, have minimal choice at the incarnate, personality level?' and 'Do I really decide what I want to do in life or am I secretly or subtly manipulated by some great chess player in the sky?'

When we ask such questions we are seeking meaning in life and to put ourselves in some sort of context in the world and in the wider life around us. Although for most of us working for a home, a career and a family life is important, for many of us these things alone are not enough. We seek another, wider context.

In every age, every culture and at every time, there have also been those who shun the material values of society and for differing reasons find various ways of going into retreat, religious or otherwise, living lives of selfless and dedicated service or opting out of the common round. Many, however, believe in, and long for, another dimension that exists within and alongside the life of every day and brings inspiration, fulfilment and a real sense of purpose, and transcends the extremes between retreat and total absorption in, or boredom with, material values.

The job we do is bound to be more congenial if there is job satisfaction or if it allows us to exercise our particular gifts or skills. For many the job that is undertaken from a place of real choice will either have an element of service or clear value in terms of doing something for others, for the community or for the environment, or it will be linked to the expression of an obvious or known skill or gift. It can be easier to know our directions if we *are* gifted in a particular way or have a particular passion for art, literature, science, healing or teaching. If our talents or areas of personal expertise are less clearly defined, the question 'What exactly is it that I am meant to be doing?' can be asked with increasing frustration or even desperation.

C. G. Jung, the groundbreaking psychologist, observed that one of the most common reasons for people seeking counselling or psychotherapy, who were neither mentally ill nor severely neurotic, was a 'discontent with being normal'. Life without spark, fire or rapture can bring on differing degrees of 'sickness of soul'. Feeling sick of soul may take the form of apparent depression, lack of direction or the need to find a framework for living.

Religion, philosophy and psychology

Traditionally, when we want to find understanding, meaning or a wider context in life, we turn to religion, philosophy or psychology.

Religion offers us morals, creeds or rules by which to live. Priests, vicars and ministers of the church help to guide us through life's crises and to find faith and strength beyond ourselves, through prayer and a belief in God or Divine Ordinance. There is great comfort and reassurance to be found for many in the rituals, beliefs and caring structure within religion or a church.

The study of philosophy invites us to consider the 'great imponderables of life', to wonder about the world in which we live, about cosmology and relationships, our origins and purpose, the nature of order or chaos, morality and ethics, and to look into the theories and insights of the great thinkers such as Plato, Aristotle, Kant, Nietzsche or Descartes – to name but a few.

Psychology is the study by which we seek to understand ourselves and to study our behaviour patterns. By understanding the drives and constructs by which we live, collectively, racially, nationally and individually, and how we have formulated or ingested them, we seek to have a greater conscious control over our lives and decisions. Psychology works on the principle that if we understand more about the origins of the spectrum of our behaviour we can work out ways in which we might bring about positive and life-enhancing change at every level, particularly the individual and uniquely personal.

Thus we seek to understand the ingredients of positive emotional and mental health. We search for the understanding and methods by which we might move from patterns of depression, over-anxiety or underachievement to greater contentment, calmness and realisation of potential. Through greater awareness of our reaction patterns to the various influences in our lives we explore ways of freeing ourselves from old conditioning so that we can become more motivated or assertive, less angry or aggressive, less self-effacing, less or more controlling or more balanced in our relationship to ourselves and to others. (See also Further Reading, my book *Your Spiritual Journey*.)

Psychology can be highly scientific or clinical in its orientation, seeking to understand all our basic functions and drives as well as the changes that occur in us as we move from childhood, through adolescence and adulthood to old age. Beyond the purely scientific and behavioural studies of ourselves, psychology can also be very close to the fields of religion, philosophy or spirituality and can serve to form valuable bridges or interfaces between all the different ways of understanding ourselves and seeking to live our lives in full health and with satisfaction and integrity.

Modern psychological writers, such as James Hillman, Thomas Moore, John Heron or Ken Wilber, believe that in order to heal ourselves individually and collectively we need to reconnect with 'soul', myth, imagination, dreamtime, archetypes and symbols. This is the transpersonal approach to psychology, largely pioneered by such psychologists as Carl Jung, William Maslow and Roberto Assagioli, and reflected in the work of historians such as Toynbee and poets such as T. S. Eliot.

Transpersonal psychology takes into account our drive for spirituality and meaning, and eventually helps also to make the bridge into consideration of subtle worlds and the continuity of existence.

Embracing the concepts of soul and spirit interfaces with the various religious or spiritual belief systems that believe in the presence of other subtle worlds or layers of consciousness that interpenetrate with, and have an effect on, the known, material world.

There is no scientific proof of the continuity of individual existence. Yet many, through the teachings of their religion or from a personal search for wider purpose and meaning in life, believe not only in life after death but also life *before* death and the concept of reincarnation. (See also Further Reading, my book *Karma and Reincarnation* where I discuss the implications of the belief in living for many lifetimes and also explore the laws of cause and effect.)

Such credence leads to a need to know what form life beyond life may take and highlights further our need to explore what relationship our present lives have to a wider context or plan. If we are links in a far greater chain of continuing consciousness, knowing whether there is something specific we are meant to be doing with our lives becomes an even more pressing question and increases our desire to 'get it right' .

The search for guidance is inevitably linked to the search for approval. As human beings we long to know whether we are 'doing OK' or not. We can be extremely vulnerable to any suggestion that we might be getting it wrong or deviating from the approved path. The belief that we have been flung out of paradise and are all carriers of 'original sin' can be an exceedingly powerful one in our collective conditioning. The journey of evolution is most often seen as a 'journey to perfection or goodness'. The accompanying belief pattern to this tenet is that we are being continually judged or assessed for ultimate punishment or reward. Inevitably, our parents, teachers, and the political leaders of our times become linked to judgement of our behaviour and to the patterns to which we feel we *ought* to conform.

Esoteric spirituality

A belief in other planes or dimensions leads to a further field of belief and study, linked in many ways to philosophy, religion or psychology, contributing to and drawing from these fields but also existing in its own right. It is what I often term 'the field of esoteric spirituality' and it gives rise to many groups and approaches which often carry somewhere in their titles the word 'spiritual' or 'spiritualist'.

The common purpose in such groups is to seek communication with other subtler worlds and the beings or intelligences that inhabit them. These worlds and beings are able to interpenetrate with our manifest, material world, and some people, such as mediums, shamans, gurus and spiritual leaders, are thought to be gifted with the ability to contact these planes and bring messages and information from them and about them.

Religion teaches us to seek communication and inspiration through prayer and praise to the Divine. It trains or chooses priests or mediators to help us learn the art of prayer for guidance, support, the uplifting of spirit and as a means of receiving Divine inspiration and comfort. There have always been mystics within the Christian

Church who speak of an ecstatic connection with other worlds and the Light of the Divine presence. Some, such as Hildegaard von Bingen and Julian of Norwich, have given inspired teachings and writings that have brought comfort to many through the years and still do so today.

It is not necessarily easy to find or build a bridge between conventional religion and the esoteric field, but today many people and groups endeavour to do so.

The esoteric field includes the world of mediumship and channelling. It is the field that embraces communication with Spirit Guides. Gildas, my personal guide, has become reasonably well known through his teachings given in my workshops and used as inspiration for our books. There have long been other well-known Guides in the esoteric field, such as White Eagle, White Bull, Silver Birch, Helio Arkonaphous, Chan, Emmanuel and many more.

Most of these, like Gildas, are channelled by people who give a considerable proportion of their lives to the work and who, as well as bringing through the general teachings of these Guides, offer private sessions in which guidance is channelled for individuals seeking personal help from a wider dimension.

The word 'channelling', used to describe the process by which guidance from other worlds is received, is more commonly used in present times than the word 'mediumship'. The word 'medium' often has associations with the end of the last century and beginning of this, when séances, trance states, table rapping and ectoplasm were in vogue. Undoubtedly many people witnessed some amazing phenomena, but equally undoubtedly there was much faking and showmanship, which tended to throw the world of séance and spiritualism into disrepute.

It is commonly thought that all individuals who are mediumistic, or who can channel, can automatically make contact with those family members and people dear to us who have died. In fact this sort of work is a specialised area of mediumship and there are relatively few people now who practise in this way.

The word 'channelling' is not just an alternative word for

mediumship. More and more people are beginning to realise that it is an art that can be learned to some degree by most individuals who wish to do so. It depends less upon, and seeks less to produce, phenomena or evidence of survival. Most channellers will channel one Guide, or at the most, two, and focus mainly in the areas of teaching, healing, guidance and personal spiritual growth.

Channelling is associated with contacting beings from other worlds and working with Spirit Guides who can see a different perspective and guide, teach and inspire us. More and more people, though, are looking to include a degree of channelling in their daily lives, seeking guidance from a higher self, inner wisdom, or from angelic beings as well as from specific and named discarnate Spirit Guides. There is evidence of a return to the world of the imagination, which includes a belief in fairies, gnomes, angels, daemons (see Glossary) and access to intrapersonal communication as well as to different levels or layers of interpersonal communication.

In many ways, channelling is a form of inspiration. When we understand it more broadly in this way, we can see that artists, writers, poets, musicians, actors and inspirational world leaders in some way channel 'the muse'. It is important to keep this wider definition of channelling well in mind because if you want to learn how to work with your Spirit Guides it is important to be broad in your approach to what channelling is.

With Gildas, I make a slight shift of consciousness and am able to receive his words streaming into my awareness, almost like dictation. I then write those words down, or speak them on to a tape. Gildas is mainly a teaching guide and obviously the way in which I receive and transmit his communication is convenient. Many other channellers that I know, who work with groups and individuals on a more or less professional basis, work in similar, though always unique, ways.

The speaking or writing of coherent guidance whilst in an altered state of consciousness, however, is by no means the one and only way of receiving guidance and channelling for self or others. It must certainly not be held too rigidly as a model of how channelling should be. Drawing, painting, inner knowing, receiving of symbols, images, keywords or phrases, being taken on inner journeys and the dreaming of incubated dreams can all be forms of channelling. Valuing the form of receiving guidance that you may most readily access is an important aspect in finding your own unique and personal connection to your Spirit Guide. Indeed, when you consider the broadness of the spectrum of ways in which guidance can be received, although you may not yet be aware of a guidance being or presence, you may exclaim: 'But I already get guidance in this way, on a regular basis.'

Once you can say that, then it may mean only some slight changes of focus or mindset, before you are confidently enjoying the ability to channel your own guidance, philosophy and a fuller awareness of the loving, friendly, beneficent presence of your personal guide.

How our Guides help us

This chapter has begun to look at our need and quest for guidance and the beliefs that may lead us to seek such guidance from other beings or intelligences who occupy a coherent subtle world that interpenetrates with our everyday, mundane, manifest or material world. We shall move on to look at what the Guides teach and how they help us. First though, in order to illustrate the dilemmas of choice and purpose that we as normal human beings can find difficult to resolve, here are two case histories. They are intended to highlight how guidance can lead us to a comfortable certainty about our choices without categorically making those choices for us or giving us a 'read out' of our future life.

Karen's story: the dilemma of choice
My Guide Gildas was consulted by Karen about one of the most common but nevertheless difficult dilemmas of choice that may face us in life. She was in a turmoil of potential guilt, resentment and anger. It seemed that whatever choice she made in her present situation, there was going to be suffering, deprivation or blame. She felt

that life was being rather unfair to her, or putting her under unfair pressures.

Years previously Karen had gone through a divorce when her only child was quite young and had taken on the major responsibility in bringing up her daughter. Karen had not found, and also felt she did not want, a further stable relationship. Once her daughter was old enough to have a life of her own, Karen had moved abroad to do a job she loved, which involved managing a hotel and treatment spa in Spain, as part of a small company she had formed with friends. The project was flourishing. She was meeting interesting people. She relished life in a sunny climate and felt free after her years of being a single parent, which although fulfilling had still meant surviving all the challenges, difficulties and ties of bringing up a child alone.

About six years prior to Karen's consultation with Gildas, her father had died after several years of being a semi-invalid. Her mother had adjusted well to her loss, made the decision to sell the family house and had gone to live in sheltered accommodation in the same village where she and Karen's father had lived for many years. She had always had many friends and leisure interests and a full life of her own and this now continued. She was still able to travel out to Spain to see Karen from time to time, and whenever Karen was back in England she visited her mother and took her on some interesting outings. There was good continuing contact between them. Although they had never been particularly close as mother and daughter, in these latter years, perhaps because they were seeing each other relatively rarely, they had been able to enjoy an easier companionship than had been possible earlier.

The dilemma, now brought by Karen for consultation with Gildas, had been developing gradually but had suddenly escalated. Doreen, Karen's mother, had been becoming more and more forgetful and now the warden of the sheltered accommodation where she lived had contacted Karen's brother, Joshua, who lived in England with his wife and family, and said that she doubted that Doreen could survive safely for much longer in the relatively independent climate of sheltered accommodation. The warden saw signs that Doreen was not caring for herself, was deteriorating mentally and in danger of possibly causing a fire in her accommodation, having actually set off the smoke alarms three times in one week by forgetting pans on the cooker.

Karen's brother lived on the other side of England, but had made the journey to their mother's home to assess the situation. He could not but agree with the warden of the sheltered accommodation. Doreen needed more care. There had always been a strong antipathy between Doreen and Joshua's wife, Kate, and now Joshua felt it would not be fair to try to persuade her to offer Doreen a home. Although they had a large house, they had four teenage children still at home and space was therefore limited. They also knew that there would be inevitable clashes of interest between the needs of Doreen and the needs of the teenagers.

Joshua, and Kate, had begun to put pressure on Karen to return to England and take on the task of caring for Doreen. When Karen said that she did not want to give up her present lifestyle and that it was not practical for Doreen to go to Spain to be cared for, Joshua had accused Karen of being 'selfish'. Joshua's wife, Kate, had told Karen: 'You have no ties now, there is no reason why you should not look after your mother, and if you won't that means that you leave us no choice and we shall have to.' She had gone on to say, in no uncertain terms, how unfair she felt that to be for herself and her family, especially knowing that, eventually, there would almost certainly be a similar dilemma arising with her own parents, and in that case she, as an only child, would have little alternative when it came to caring for them.

'Unfairness' was a word that was coming very much to the fore, from both sides. Karen felt confused, angry and to some extent guilty. She was stung by the accusation of being selfish but wondered if there was any truth in it. Should she be putting her own needs first when her mother was in crisis? She had pointed out to Kate that because she didn't want to look after Doreen it did not necessarily mean that she felt Kate and Joshua had to. There were other alternatives and she would be happy to contribute to the costs of professional care.

All in all, although Karen knew that Gildas would not tell her exactly what to do, she felt that a wider, more spiritual view on her dilemma would help her to get a perspective as she tried to make the 'right' decision. Her questions to Gildas were: 'Can you see if it is part of my life's duty or purpose to give up all I presently hold dear in order to look after my mother? Is there some spiritual obligation or karmic debt that I should know about or take into account? In your [Gildas's] general spiritual overview of things, does duty or honour towards one's parents mean, emphatically, that sacrifices should be made in order to ensure their welfare? And if so, why should I be the one to make that sacrifice rather than my brother and family?'

Gildas always begins a consultation of this kind with the words: 'In replying to your questions and commenting on your present life situation, I shall be looking at those subtle energy lines and patterns around you that enable me to give you a wider spiritual and evolutionary picture.' From these subtle energy lines and patterns, he is able to see whether there is some ongoing situation between people or in their life's purposes or 'contract' that might affect the basis on which they make a decision or choice at any given time.

In his reply to Karen, Gildas linked her question about life's duty and purpose to the one about karma and/or spiritual obligation. He said that he could not see any karmic link between Karen and Doreen that might have indicated that she 'owed' anything more to Doreen than the normal honouring of any daughter for her mother. He felt though, that when making her choice, Karen had to be careful that she did not do anything that would make her resent her mother because of her needs. If that happened, he said, then she might be *putting* Doreen into the position of having karmic debt or 'unfinished business' to clear up with Karen in some future state or lifetime. Therefore, whatever Karen chose, whatever contribution she made to her mother's future quality of life, she needed to be sure that she was able to give freely. Sacrifice would not necessarily be virtuous or right unless it could be made wholeheartedly, with 'if onlys' put aside. (See also Further Reading, my book *Karma and Reincarnation*.)

Gildas advised Karen to look heart-searchingly at the 'if only' aspect. He asked her to try to imagine each choice she might make and then to see herself at her mother's deathbed or funeral. With each choice available to her, at the end, there might be an 'if only'. Gildas reminded her that she, Karen, would most likely be living on long after her mother had died and suggested she look at which 'if only' she would find it easiest to live with and accept.

He then spoke to her, as he speaks to many people, about 'responsibility to' and 'responsibility for'. His spiritual viewpoint states that human beings are responsible *to* each other but not *for* each other, we are only responsible *for* ourselves and for very young children. To be responsible *to* another person means that we help and support them to the best of our ability without trying to control, direct or rescue them. If we consider ourselves to be responsible *for* another person, it might mean that we take over too much and compromise their choices. To be responsible for ourselves means that we take responsibility for our own quality of life, so as not to overburden others with any sense that we have curtailed our own interests in order to serve theirs, unless we can truly give such service with a singing heart.

Gildas also suggested that Doreen's view of her future should be ascertained. He said that although Doreen was no longer as fully present in her mind and thoughts as she had once been, she was still capable of having an opinion about arrangements for her future care and that she should be consulted rather than the family trying to take responsibility for her in such a way as to offer her no choice, but a *fait accompli*.

After the session Karen said that she felt that Gildas had subtly confirmed her sense that just when she had established for herself a regime she loved, she should not necessarily be expected to give it up or to demand of herself that she give it up in order to be her mother's carer. She saw that all kinds of her own and her brother's emotions were not being fully expressed. They were facing up to the 'end of an era' in a way that had not been necessary when their father died, because their mother had made many strong decisions at that time. Karen felt that she could tell Joshua and Kate quite unequiv-ocally that she was not prepared to devote the next phase of her life to looking after her mother and that this decision certainly did not mean that she therefore expected them to step in as carers. She would suggest to them that they should research a choice of suitable care establishments, discuss what financial contribution each was prepared to make, should it be necessary, and then leave the choice of location to Doreen.

In the event, when Joshua and Karen chose what they felt was a good moment to speak to Doreen about her future, she immediately said, 'I don't want either of you to change your lives in order to look after me.' She had already decided that when the time came she would go to a professional care home. Earlier, she had even made some preliminary research herself into what kind of care might be available in the area where she now lived and knew of one place where she could have an attractive room with a view and where she felt the caring atmosphere was kindly. She was also open to looking at other places and locations.

Eventually Joshua said that a good compromise for him would be if a care home of the right kind could be found within a short distance of where he now lived. Then he could visit frequently and feel he was making a contribution of regular contact that Karen would not be able to make. A good 'rest home' was found, and when Doreen visited it she felt that she could live happily there with the bonus of this regular contact with Joshua and Kate, and, for at least a while longer, the grandchildren who she had seen less frequently than she would have liked.

So, a decision in which everyone felt they had a part was made. Joshua later confided in Karen that he would actually have felt extremely guilty if she *had* changed her life so dramatically in order to care for Doreen. And Karen said that when she was absolutely honest with herself the most painful 'if only' she saw herself feeling when she contemplated the end of Doreen's life was 'if only I had not cut myself off from a life full of opportunity that it is now too late to go back to'. She saw that she could not have avoided feeling resentment towards Doreen if that had been the action she felt compelled to take.

Doreen lived for another three years, well cared for in a kind and unchanging environment which helped her to feel more secure and more 'in touch' for as long as possible. On her death, the whole family felt there was a clarity and acceptance between them that might not have been there if they had pursued the path they were on the point of pursuing when Karen came for consultation.

Anthony's story: the dilemma of purpose in life
In transpersonal psychology the age of 42 is often seen as a time when big life changes might be made. Anthony was 42 years old, married with two children, a boy of twelve and a girl of eight when he came to consult Gildas.

Some of Anthony's issues were similar to those that Karen had been so perplexed about. They involved loyalty to parents, but in Anthony's case they concerned whether he should be loyal to his parents' vision of his career and purpose in life or whether he should strike out on his own and start a new life phase that he felt would give him a greater sense of creativity, challenge and of being or becoming his 'true self'.

Since before Anthony was born his parents had owned an ever-growing and thriving garage and car sales business on the edge of a small town in one of the more prosperous areas of Britain. As well-known business people in a small town, they had many friends and a good quality of business and social life. Anthony was an only son and it had always been assumed that at the appropriate age he would take his place as a full partner in the firm. When he finished school, Anthony had taken some business management training and had indeed joined his father's firm and helped to update some of the procedures within it and to keep it well 'on the map' in terms of modern trading requirements. As well as business training he had also served a full apprenticeship on the mechanical side of the work and was known in the business to be a clever mechanical problem solver. He was practical and astute. But now he said: 'I am bored! I am bored with the daily procedures. I am bored now that the business has, in many ways, reached its ultimate potential and there is no further to go unless we consider opening other branches elsewhere. I am bored with conforming with and fulfilling my parents' image of how my life should be.'

Anthony's wife, Rowena, was aware of his discontent, but his parents were not. They were proud of their business successes and particularly of the part that Anthony had played in keeping these up to date. They felt that they had given Anthony and his family a real heritage for the future. They got on well with Rowena and doted on their grandchildren. The business, family and the status they enjoyed in the small town where they lived, plus the prospect of the security of all they had achieved continuing and being passed down from father to son and to grandchildren, gave them a great sense of contentment.

Anthony was far from content and had come to dread what he felt was the treadmill of his, and perhaps even his son's and daughter's, future, all carefully mapped out before them. In some ways he felt trapped by security and certainly by the expectations that his parents had for him and, increasingly, by the position he was expected to fulfil in small town life.

Anthony's vision was of taking very early semi-retirement so that he could move close to the sea. He wanted to try to fulfil an ambition to write, which, though he had never had anything published, had long been an active hobby for him. Alongside this, he had a great interest in the sea and boats and felt that if he lived near enough to a marina he could service boat engines and supply parts. Because his parents' business had thrived so consistently and because of their financial prudence and generosity and some wise investments, Anthony was in a financial position to take certain risks and to contemplate earning comparatively little for a while.

Since their marriage, Rowena had not really needed to work outside the home, but before meeting Anthony she had achieved some success as an illustrator and had continued to pursue her own career to her own satisfaction. It was work that she could do from almost any location. She felt that living near the sea would be a lovely thing to do and would perhaps bring health benefits for them all. The children were at the ages where, if they moved fairly quickly, it would not be too difficult to make a change of schools, but if the decision were to be delayed, then that issue alone would make Anthony need to think again.

In his comments on Anthony's dilemma and questions, Gildas pointed out that his decision, in many ways, was already made. He just needed the 'permission' and courage to put his plans for his own future to his parents and the support to cope with their inevitable disappointment.

Gildas also spoke about the human need to find the 'true self' rather than the 'conditioned self'. Anthony had been continually endeavouring to live out the expectations of his parents, the future to which he had been conditioned, the purpose which they had mapped out for him. He was not really a manager or a mechanic, by nature. Neither of these pursuits gave room for his imagination or literary bent. His identification was much more with 'The Writer' but he got little enough opportunity to pursue his passion or to find inspiration for his creativity. He had proved that he could run a business well, but his success had seemed to stifle rather than to satisfy his true inner being.

Gildas also pointed out that once there was an emergence of an urge to fulfil something other in life than that which was currently being pursued, it could be threatening to physical health to ignore it. When conformity wins out over vision or inspiration then the physical body may find it difficult to maintain optimum health. (See also Further Reading, my book *Energy Healing for Beginners*.)

It always takes courage to make radical change but especially so when you are aware that it will deeply affect the lives of others. At the end of his session Anthony saw that there were many reasons why he had to be true to himself and somehow break the news of his new life plans to his parents, and he felt determined to do so.

I did not hear of Anthony again for another two years, until he attended one of my courses held in the area in which he was now living. He had followed his vision and had even found that his parents' reaction to his news was quite different from what he had expected. They were secretly also becoming a little weary of the daily round and the constant need to 'keep up appearances'. They wondered whether Anthony and Rowena would mind if they moved near to the place where they were looking to live, in order to keep up the close contact they had all always enjoyed. The business sold well, and Anthony's parents found a village that was neither too close nor too far from Anthony and Rowena and where they could build up the kind of social contacts that would enable them to continue to pursue a number of their favourite community interests and activities.

Anthony was enjoying the process of continuing to find his true self, the children had settled well into their new schools, Rowena loved walking the dog on the cliffs near their new home and also found the new environment stimulating for her own work. A successful outcome had been achieved.

About two years later I received a complementary copy of Anthony's first novel that he had been successful in getting published and which was receiving some distinct acclaim.

Within these case histories there is some evidence of a particular philosophy or wisdom about life that Spirit Guides tend to teach or on which they tend to base their advice and encouragement to us. It is based on that fascinating blend of psychology, spirituality and philosophy that is the bridge and the interface between our world and theirs. The next chapter will go on to discuss this in greater detail, partly with the aim of building up a fuller sense of what to expect from your own true Guides if/when you choose to endeavour to have more contact with them.

2

What Spirit Guides Teach

This chapter explores the philosophy of our Spirit Guides and gives a working cosmology or overview of the plan, purpose and process of evolution, including reference to soul, spirit, higher self and twin souls. A basic understanding of these concepts and the philosophy that enfolds them helps us understand the dimension from which our Guides come and the perspective they will endeavour to give us to help us in living our lives more meaningfully.

Do all Spirit Guides say the same things?

One of Gildas's favourite and central teachings is entitled 'The Many Faceted Jewel of Truth'. He uses this image to try to help us to modify our search for 'absolute truth'. The whole jewel is only complete with all its facets, but at any given moment you can see into the centre of the jewel only through a few of the facets. If you turn the jewel you see other views of the centre and of the jewel itself. Some facets are in direct opposition to others, yet they are all necessary to the beauty of the whole.

In Western scientific logic we have become used to severe categorisation, but even modern scientific paradigms are now changing to include the position from which several points of view can be true at one and the same time depending on the angle of perception.

A Belgian friend who wrote the introduction to my book *Working with your Chakras* (see Further Reading) included in that introduction the following story:

> An old Indian priest told me how to see these paradoxes: 'Suppose that between you and me there are three towers. Two of the towers are standing on one axis. The third one is standing out of the axis. Now I ask you, "Where does the third tower stand? On your right or left side?" You will say for instance:
> "On the right side." But for me that will be on the left, or vice versa.'

If we keep this in mind, we gradually learn that although Spirit Guides may have different ways of saying things and may take slightly different approaches to our problems, one piece of given advice or information very rarely negates another but rather will complement it. Guides rarely say categorically 'this' or 'that' but often 'and/and'. Whilst we see difficult choices, black and white patterns, or the necessity to choose one thing and leave another behind, Guides will often show us how to be creative and even how to make a lie of the old adage 'you can't have your cake and eat it'.

A working cosmology

In meeting with, working with and listening to many Guides communicating through different channels there is common reference to a certain model of the cosmos. Although there may be some differences according to the facet of the jewel of truth that is being presented, most Spirit Guides seem to subscribe to a similar explanation of the intricacies of cosmology.

This view, without exception in my experience, includes the concepts of karma and reincarnation and the living of many lifetimes in order to gain the experience that leads to evolution. There are three main interactive aspects that give meaning, purpose, organisation and context to our lives. These are soul, spirit and higher self, and most Guides speak frequently of them.

Many people believe that it is the soul that incarnates, but most

Spirit Guides teach us that it is actually the spirit that illuminates, vitalises and is totally present within our incarnate beings, whilst the soul observes and oversees.

The higher self is an aspect of soul that carries and interprets the growing body of knowledge and wisdom that is acquired by living incarnate lives. It organises our pattern of incarnation and evolution and decides what kind of incarnation is needed or necessary for the continuation of our eternal learning process. When we die, our spirit or essence returns to the soul stem or thread so that the learning from any given lifetime can be integrated with the learning or experience from other lifetimes. When our need for learning through incarnation is over, soul and spirit are totally reunited. The image often given for this reunification is that of the chalice of the soul containing the flame of the spirit in the ultimate mystical marriage.

Allied to soul, spirit and higher self are twin souls, soul family, kindred souls and soul mates. Knowing more about these helps to explain why we get on with, or feel more connected to some people we meet in incarnation better than with others.

For the start of the evolution of each one of us, Gildas gives the analogy of a spark emanating out from a Divine Source to begin the journey of experience that will eventually lead to reunification with that Source. The journey is necessary so that things do not become static, with human beings as pure innocents dependent on the Source as provider, parent, teacher, authority and judge. We start out on the journey of evolution as naïve innocents, but before our eventual return to the Source we learn to understand ourselves as wise innocents who are co-creators of, and within, the cosmos.

The original spark, for reasons of economy in the gaining of experience, splits into two. Imagery is important in describing the complex workings of the process of evolution and in helping us to come to some sort of coherent understanding of it. Thus from the point where the original spark splits, a common analogy is of two ears of wheat on the same stem, separate in themselves but sharing a common root. The core of each ear holding the grains is a soul. Ears sharing a common root are twin souls.

Each ear of wheat undertakes a somewhat different journey, which is governed not only by the laws of karma, or cause and effect, but also, most importantly, by the need to gain a wide experience of life and living in order to become fully conscious and responsible for our actions within the cosmos. This consciousness can only come to fruition through a journey of many lifetimes. The grains on the ears of wheat represent the many lifetimes that may be lived. The stalks that hold the ears of wheat are the soul stems; the core that holds the grains is the higher self who governs the main purposes of each incarnation.

Twin souls

In life, we all long to meet our twin soul, the one who shares our common root, the other half of our original spark. Many questions to Guides are about the potential for meeting our twin souls and about advice as to whether an important meeting or partnership in our lives can be interpreted as a true unification with this dear and complementary 'half' of our original spark. We seek a sense of completion and belonging, and feel that if only we could be guided to such a meeting or have it arranged for us all would be well.

Apparently in some eras of human history, such as some dynasties in ancient Egypt and some eras of Native American experience, it was more common for twin souls to be together, in harmony, in incarnation. However, another teaching Spirit Guides have in common, which needs to be iterated for us now, concerns our swiftly moving times. Most Spirit Guides seem to agree that we are on the edge of a major change, with a lot to be accomplished in order that humanity may take a quantum leap towards realising our ultimate potential, not only as individuals but also collectively.

Since twin souls gain experience from a common root, it can be that taking a similar journey or enjoying the bliss of that special mutual companionship is counter-productive in a demanding phase of development such as we live in today. Thus, Gildas and other Spirit Guides tell us that in the present times it is relatively rare to have that sort of connection with our twin souls and that they are often not incarnate at the same time as us. If we do meet them, the possibility for a relationship can be surrounded by obstacles, challenges and steep learning curves. We may have to accept that although our twin souls are incarnate at the same time as we are, being together has to be sacrificed or perhaps achieved only at a great price.

The overall purpose of evolution

So although grains from both ears of wheat from the same stem may incarnate at the same time, they will, especially in our present times, seek to have complementary or different experiences so that greater knowledge can be added to the composite soul stem. This adding of greater knowledge and experience is the overall purpose of evolution. We are not trying to get better and better and pass exams set by some higher authority. We are aiming to broaden our experience until we are in a true place of choice.

In his teachings to groups, Gildas often iterates his view that there are no wrong choices. Our fears about 'not getting it right' are usually groundless. Our souls and higher selves need us to gain breadth of experience, rather than to 'get it right'. We all, who are incarnate, know that there are many crossroads in life but few clear signposts. This is because, in many ways, it does not matter which turning we take. Each road will lead to a different experience. Each choice we make is important to our higher selves only because it leads to experience.

The pre-birth choices of our souls, such as choice of parents, gender, type of body, genetic inheritance, geographical place of incarnation, historical era of incarnation and social milieu of incarnation, provide a certain limitation to the territory of choice whilst still leaving us with a broad spectrum of choices to be made in the course of life. Thus, within the territory of choice, unless we deliberately and knowingly choose to do something destructive, manipulative or even premeditatively evil, there are no wrong choices – only learning opportunities.

The paths of wholeness and perfection

Spirit Guides usually tell us that we are on a path of wholeness, not a path of perfection. It is experience and the growth of wisdom that is important in our evolution, not 'making the grade' or 'getting it right'. Questions to Guides that include 'shoulds' or 'oughts' belong to the concept of the path of perfection and usually need to be rephrased. Responses from Spirit Guides that contain the words 'should' and 'ought' are the kind of responses of which we may need to be wary (see also Chapter 4).

Karma and reincarnation

To some extent karma and reincarnation include the mechanisms of cause and effect. But the oft-quoted 'law' of karma 'as ye sow so shall ye reap' is incomplete and over-simplistic. Karma is about learning, not about punishment – especially not about punishment meted out by some higher authority. (See also Further Reading, my book *Karma and Reincarnation* for more detailed information on karma as a concept.)

I as I am now, and you as you are now, in this present lifetime, have never incarnated before and will never incarnate again. We are one of the grains of wheat on the ear of wheat on our soul stem. When we return to the soul stem, taking the experiences we have gathered in this life with us, another personality grain from the ear of wheat will take up the causes and effects we may have created and will seek to broaden incarnate experience. Such a subsequent incarnating personality may also seek to continue work we have begun or to redeem imbalances we have created. Such purposes or 'menus' for incarnation are created by our higher selves. Our personal Spirit Guides are close to our higher selves and understand our higher, overall purposes. As part of guidance and teaching for us, they will help us to interpret these purposes and so make more spiritually informed decisions in our lives.

As we finish one lifetime, the next grain to incarnate from our ear of wheat may take on an opposite polarity lifetime from the one that has just been lived. So, if we have been clever or rich or poor or ordinary, male or female, the next personality grain to incarnate may be the opposite. The subsequent incarnating grain after the polarity lives will probably have a task of finding a balance between the polarities. In this way, causes we set in motion through being too much one thing or too little another are taken care of and an understanding of balance is gradually achieved. We 'choose' parents, siblings and partners, sometimes because they are close to us at a soul level, but also sometimes because they will give us the challenges that make us more conscious of, and more personally responsible for, our choices and decisions.

If then, we stay with the analogy of grains of wheat on an ear of wheat on a stem which bears two ears of wheat and has a common root, we come to understand that not only do we have twin souls, but that the grains on our own ear of wheat are not only soul family, but other aspects of our soul, united in the task of evolution. Each incarnating grain carries the 'baton' for the continuous process of gaining that wealth of experience that leads to wholeness.

Linguistically, when we speak about past lives and reincarnation it is easier or simpler to say: 'When I was in Egypt in another lifetime ...'; we also need to remember, however, that although we may have a shared memory of that lifetime, it was not us as we are now that had that experience, but another personality grain on the ear of wheat that is our total and complex soul.

Understanding the basic structures

I have gone into some detail here about these basic structures that Spirit Guides use in order to teach and guide us, because I believe that when we understand in this way we cease to seek clairvoyant prediction or to persist in the belief that our lives are totally mapped out for us and even cease to want them to be so. Most Spirit Guides dislike questions, for example, that begin: 'Am I *meant* to get married?', 'Am I *meant* to be an artist?', and particularly, 'What am I *meant* to be doing with my life?'

Such questions imply that we see ourselves as pieces on some kind of chessboard, or as actors on a vast world stage playing out our roles with no personal choice or responsibility for our life script. Guides teach us to take responsibility for our own actions and for making those choices that will enable our own futures to become more creative and satisfying. We need to learn to ask our Guides to support us and show us how to empower ourselves, rather than wanting them to make the path totally smooth for us in some way.

Certain openings in life may indeed be blocked for us in various ways, but understanding that those blockages are there in order to help us to 'keep on an evolutionary course', which means working for the total evolutionary experience of our complex souls, helps us to accept them and to appreciate the many other openings that are always there for us.

With an initial basic understanding of the philosophies and structure that underlie the guidance and insights that Spirit Guides can give, we can move on to look at some questions often asked about Guides and guidance.

3

Questions Often Asked about Spirit Guides

Learning about the existence of Spirit Guides is bound to fill us with curiosity and sometimes fear. What can, can't and maybe shouldn't Spiritual Guides do or say? We may have many questions to ask before we decide to pursue the path of making a personal relationship with our own Guides through the exercises given in subsequent chapters. Through revisiting questions Gildas and I have been asked frequently over the years I hope to increase your information about the nature and purpose of Spirit Guides and the worlds from which they come. The chapter ends with Amanda's story, which considers the nature of false guidance. Meanwhile, perhaps the most frequently asked questions are:

Do we all have Spirit Guides?

Many Spirit Guides, especially those who were channelled in the earlier years of the twentieth century, have spoken of a Great White Brotherhood whose members exist in the other worlds or more subtle dimensions of life and who are there for the purpose of guiding us. Our personal, true Spirit Guides are usually members of this shining company of discarnates. If we genuinely seek to have contact with our personal Spirit Guide and are able to learn to be open to that contact in safety, then a being is there for us.

Some of this company of Guides seek a more general connection with incarnate humanity, and may be channelled by more than one incarnate human being. It is possible as you learn to channel that you might 'tap in' to one of these more universal Guides, but you will always find that there is someone there for you who is personally spiritually connected to you and your higher self.

Are they all male?

Today, with our awareness in society of 'political correctness' and male–female equality of opportunity, the use of language that describes the world of spirit can seem to err on the side of male supremacy and the paternal model. Beyond the Great White Brotherhood, or at a certain level of it, we are also told that there are Ascended Masters. Part of the joy of my conscious and cooperative contact with Gildas is that I can make him aware of issues like political correctness in our times! He once joked that he knew that speaking of Ascended Masters might not be PC but that it would probably be equally inappropriate to speak of Ascended Mistresses! He usually resolves these issues in his communications now by speaking of the Great White Company and the Ascended Ones for, indeed, not all Spirit Guides or ascended higher beings are male.

Many teaching Guides are male whilst healing Guides are more frequently female and often refer to themselves as 'Sisters of Mercy'. In many senses the Guides are beyond personality and gender. They have lived many lifetimes and even though they now inhabit the timeless dimension, they carry a long history of incarnate and discarnate knowledge and experience. Quite a number of communicating Guides speak of having been in incarnation in Atlantean times.

Most Spirit Guides say that they are now in a state where they no longer need to reincarnate. In their present state of existence they are more diffuse entities than we can be as incarnate beings. Their bodies are light or energy bodies and when they contact us wearing a specific 'costume' they are, for our benefit, picking up a wavelength that they feel will be most easily perceptible to us, and putting on a less subtle appearance in order to make what Gildas has termed 'a strong and tender contact'.

All my life, I have had an affinity for most things French. When Gildas revealed himself to me in the monastic robe of his final incarnation as a Benedictine monk in fourteenth-century France, there was something about that wavelength and that era that made me feel comfortable with such an image. Now, I rarely see Gildas in his monk's robe, because I have learned to pick him up clearly on his energy wavelength. I sense his nearness, and at the moment when he is ready to communicate, I see him as a shimmering colour and smell him as a fragrance.

As I discussed in my introduction on page ix, Gildas does not want to be identified with any Gildas who lived in the fourteenth century as a monk. He feels that such identification limits him too much and places him too strongly within our linear historical model. He is in the 'now' even more than we are in the now and presumably could have appeared to me in a number of different guises related to his experience in previous lives.

Have we known our Spirit Guides before?

Within the system of soul, soul group and higher self, we all have personal Guides, helpers and guardian angels of either gender, who watch over us and help us towards synchronicity and opportunity in life. Some of these will associate themselves with the Great White Company and others will tell us that they are close soul group 'relatives' – helping us and helping the progress of our souls and soul groups.

Spirit Guides are evolved beings. They will have some close spiritual or soul level link to us, but being a Guide is their 'job'. They are helping us and watching over us, whether we make a conscious effort to connect with them or not. Once we connect with them through conscious and specific effort and training we will come to know them as our best friends and wise advisers. They can then give us the benefit of wider insights and perspectives as we learn more and more about the art of cooperation with our soul purposes and the conscious management of our incarnate lives.

Some of us may feel a strong contact with people we have known in this present lifetime but who have died, such as grandparents, other relatives or wise friends. Gildas is often asked a question such as: 'I feel a strong wise presence near me and speaking to me, but it feels like my grandmother or my mother/father/uncle/husband/dear friend who died last year/ten years ago. Could my dead grand-mother/relative/friend be my Guide?'

The answer to this is affirmative because relatives we have known in life are often close to us at a soul level and many want to continue that close link with us, and care for us when they have crossed to the other side. They may particularly want to let us know that life continues. If they are experienced enough to be chosen for such work, they may well become our Guides and teachers or spiritual helpers, as at least a part of their 'occupation' in the subtle realms.

Nevertheless, a word of caution is also necessary here, as it does not necessarily follow that because someone has died they immedi-ately become wise and detached enough to be a true Spirit Guide. Evolution continues between incarnations as well as during incarna-tions. Uncle Albert who was a dear friend in life, but not necessarily the wisest person to approach when in a dilemma, does not, just because he has crossed to the 'other side' immediately become a discerning fount of knowledge. Yet, if you sense a link of deep wisdom, love and overseeing, then of course dear ones who have died can be Guides and helpers, and can go on communicating their love, concern, guidance and watchfulness, and care for us.

Relatives apart, almost certainly we will have known our Spirit Guides before. We will have met them in some other incarnation, and perhaps in several other incarnations. We will share a deep understanding and trust with them that comes from the soul level, and they will feel like dear friends and give us a sense of home-coming and security.

Do we have more than one Spirit Guide?

We certainly can, and probably most of us do, have more than one Spirit Guide. However, in the first stages of developing closer contact with a Spirit Guide, there will be one main presence with whom to build the bridge of communication and whom it is wisest to focus on. Gildas is my main communicating Guide and I have accepted that our work is closely intertwined with all that this means for me in this present lifetime, but I *am* aware of other helpers and also of a female Guide with whom I communicate frequently but rarely publicly.

If you concentrate on, or look for, one communicating being to start with, eventually the work will take on its own momentum and you may develop a sensitivity to, or awareness of, other Guides. The importance of not being too over-enthusiastic was summed up in the succinct message that was given to one ardent seeker. He had become passionate about all psychic and spiritual phenomena. Eventually, after a number of adventures and challenges, he made a particularly clear connection to a female Guide who said: 'At last we have found each other. The contact has been more difficult to build because your search was so wide and dissipated, so my first gift to you is the gift of limitation.'

It is a classic paradox of the spiritual worlds that in our search for our Spirit Guides we need to open ourselves up as, perhaps, we have never opened ourselves before, but at one and the same time we need to do so with clear intent and focus and a respect for boundaries.

Do our Spirit Guides know when we are trying to make contact?

Our Spirit Guides do indeed know when we are trying to make contact with them, as, almost always, they are already trying to make contact with us. They may already be guiding us through our life challenges in subtle and unrecognised ways. On pages 28–9 of this chapter, I mentioned how our Spirit Guides' readiness to take on a recognisable personality for connection with us is part of their concern to make a 'strong and tender contact'. This is part of the journey they make to come towards us. This book is mainly concerned with how those of us who are longing for clear contact with Spirit Guides can learn to make our part of the journey to that safe meeting point so that a strong, conscious, two-way interaction can occur.

It does not work just to say: 'I am open to being contacted by my Spirit Guide – here I am, just speak to me.' We have to learn to raise our level of awareness, to go into a slightly altered state of consciousness and to use imagery or chakras (our personal energy centres) to maintain a focus of attention at a raised level of awareness (see Chapter 4, page 64). It is not difficult to find bridges or openings through to other planes of being and existence and the communication that comes from there, but our true Spirit Guides function from a higher level than the other planes. By requiring us to learn to travel to the subtle meeting place, or 'rainbow bridge', between the worlds, they offer us an inbuilt protection (see also Chapter 4, exercise 5, on page 64). They truly rejoice when they know that we are actively working to build the awareness necessary for this conscious communication.

How we receive guidance

The main purpose of the 'Where am I now' section of exercise 4, Chapter 4, page 61 is to help us to understand that our lives are already guided and that even before we endeavour to contact them our Guides are helping us through various coincidences and synchronicities so that we will be in the right place at the right time.

At crucial life points we make one choice rather than another. A particular set of circumstances ensures that we arrive in a certain place at a certain time, or meet a certain person at a certain time. Even accidents and illnesses may play a part in shaping the pattern of our lives. We may look back with disappointment, resentment, frustration or resignation. We may wish that 'the fates' had dealt us a better hand, but usually a definitive pattern can be observed. Life tends to guide us by knocks on the head and kicks from behind, but I am always impressed by the number of people who, having lived through extremely difficult experiences, say: 'If I could go back, I wouldn't change a thing, because I have learned and grown so much through meeting this (or that) challenge.'

To make an analogy, to some extent in life we have to play the hand of cards we have been dealt, although learning to play the cards skilfully can make a big difference to the quality and meaning of life. It is this learning that our Spirit Guides can most help us with. The knocks and challenges will still come, but with guidance perhaps they will take us less unawares and there will be fewer 'kicks from behind' as we gain access to a pertinent commentary on the things that puzzle and confuse us. Where necessary, we will have assistance in changing our attitudes, so that a more creative approach to life can blossom and more of a sense of joy and fulfilment in living can come in.

In the highest sense, whatever is happening to us, whatever place of learning or challenge we may be in, we are always in the right place at the right time. When we recognise this, we are able to see more clearly the wider guidance of the choices made for our present incarnations by our higher selves, as I discussed in Chapter 2 page 21. In addition, specific guidance, obtained by a more conscious contact with our Spirit Guides, enables and fosters the most positive use of any life experience.

Do Spirit Guides know everything?

The short answer to this is an emphatic 'No'. Of course, we may often want to believe that they know everything, but then we should also be asking the question: 'Can the whole of the future ever be known, by anyone – or at all?' Spirit Guides tell us that because of the variable factors in our relationships to each other and the challenges of life, only a certain proportion of the future can be known. We can see future *potential* clearly, but when, how and whether we

shall reach it is less known and also very much within our own juris-
diction.

There is also the complex question: 'If future things are known,
are they then automatically preordained or absolutely predestined?'
If this were so, then we would have no free will and be little more
than the puppets of some powerful ordinance.

How will knowing my Spirit Guide change my life?

Spirit Guides encourage us to see ourselves as co-creators not only
in our personal lives but also in the life of the collective and the
cosmos or universe. They also see themselves as co-creators and
part of their interaction with us is to enable their co-creativity
as well as ours.

A favourite guidance or teaching phrase that I frequently remind
myself of is: 'Nothing exists except in relationship to something
else.' Gildas tells us that quality of life is gained only by being in a
more creative relationship to all that exists. This includes our relationship to the most mundane concerns of immediate life, such as
doing the shopping and taking the dog for a walk, as well as to every
aspect of creation and existence that impinges on our awareness
now, or has ever impinged on our awareness. Changing our relationship to people and things changes our lives, and when we
change our lives we inevitably change the lives of others. When
enough people make positive changes in their lives, then everything
and everybody will change.

Although Spirit Guides can read the subtle lines and energy
patterns around each one of us, see and interpret our higher life
plans or even our higher life contracts and search the akashic
records, which give details of our previous existences, they don't, and
can't, *know* everything. However, they have access to the wisdom
that is born of experience, to knowledge about patterns and rhythms
and to a wider vision and perspective of things than we have in our
everyday lives, and they possess more finite perceptions.

Knowing Spirit Guides will change our lives in the sense that the dimension they bring to us is enriching. They will help us to see a pattern in life and to have more confidence in the choices we make, or have previously made. They will bring us a structure that enables us to put the events of our own lives, and even the things that are happening to the wider dimension of humanity, into a meaningful context. They will help us to know that we are important to the whole, just by being, and that we do not have to earn our right to existence. They will teach us that there are no mistakes – only experiential learning opportunities and challenges.

The changes that knowing our Spirit Guides make to our lives, and our ability to live them, are subtle and rarely dramatic: suggestions will be made and wider viewpoints put before us. True Guides are non-judgemental, comforting and supportive. With this comfort and support we may be inspired to make those big choices or changes we have always wanted to make, but have put on hold for various reasons, including the fear of 'getting it wrong'. A big change may come, but it should arise only as a result of the inspiration and reassurance that our Guides bring, not because of any *direction*, *absolute instruction* or *command* from them. Any Guide who tells us exactly what to do or takes over our lives is not a true Guide, or the communication has been 'coloured' (that is, there is imperfect attunement, or an emotional attachment to the results is affecting the messages that come through; see Chapter 8 page 130 for more on 'colouring' in guidance).

Will my Spirit Guide ever reincarnate?

Most dedicated Spirit Guides tell us that they have reached a place in their evolution where they no longer need to incarnate. The specific soul to which they belong is not likely to put out any more personality grains into incarnation, as I discussed in Chapter 2 pages 24–5. Their task for humanity now is one of devoted guidance – maintaining a bridge of communication between our world and theirs. In one rather dramatic communication, however, Gildas did indicate that should humanity ever reach such a point of precarious balance that we were threatening to tip into self-destruction and the destruction of our planet, a number of Guides would *instantly* incarnate in order to prevent this. However, he always reassures us that he confidently does not expect humanity ever to reach this point and that we would draw back from the real danger areas well before the self-destruct mechanism could be triggered.

Can my Spirit Guide tell me the winning lottery numbers?

If this were possible, I wonder whether I would actually be sitting here, at my computer, writing this book now. It is our own personal intuitive factors that are more likely to tell us winning numbers, football results and winning horses than our Spirit Guides. Although their wisdom helps us definitively to a better quality of life and greater awareness, they are not able to arrange or forecast absolutely everything to make our lives just the way we think we want them to be.

Could my Spirit Guide come from another planet?

There are a number of channellers today who are giving coherent and meaningful guidance that they attribute to communicators from other planets, star systems or galaxies. Humankind is inspired to send rockets, probes and satellites, manned and unmanned, into space to answer the question whether there is active life or intelligence out there in the universe wanting to communicate with us. Indeed, many people who are familiar with the sense of other dimensions and planes share a belief that there is indeed intelligence 'out there' and that it is possible to channel messages from these other beings. Once you open up to your channelling abilities, it is possible that you may eventually have such an experience if you are receptive to it. However, a communicator from another planet or star is not a Spirit Guide within the soul organisation described in Chapter 2, pages 20–1. My advice would always be first to seek contact with the Spirit Guide who is, even now, concerned with watching over you, and only later when you have more confidence and knowledge to expand into other fields, if you wish to do so. A strong, developed contact with your true Spirit Guide will support you in any future, wider explorations you want to make. However, if this particular other dimension seems to be opening for you before you feel totally confident, you might consider consulting an experienced channeller or spiritual teacher. Communicators from any other dimension, including our true Spirit Guides, should always be challenged or checked in one way or another for their integrity, as I discuss in Chapter 5, page 79. This is particularly important to remember if you ever *do* get a communication or communicator that claims to come from another star, planet or galaxy.

Do Spirit Guides believe in fun?

In my experience Spirit Guides have a tremendous sense of humour and fun. Of course, their teachings are serious and deep, but they often interject humour and teasing asides. One of my groups that meets regularly for spiritual growth and to receive Gildas's teachings has been in existence for a long time, with some founder members still regularly attending. So many individuals in the group know Gildas well and he knows them. Although, when I am channelling, I am never fully aware of what Gildas is saying, I do know, sometimes, that there is a lot of laughter and banter going on in the group, and when I read the transcripts afterwards I realise that, often with great humour, Gildas can remind or gently tease people when they slip into old or negative patterns or are blocking their own progress or opportunity.

I know several people who are also exceptionally close to their own Guides, and when we get together the Guides sometimes seem to want to join in. Nowadays it is usually only on these occasions that I see Gildas in his monkish robe and his more human form. On one occasion a friend and I were going out for a celebratory meal in London; we had decided to go by bus, rather than to drive. Our

Guides soon made it clear that they wanted to be part of this occasion and obviously enjoyed sitting in the front seats on the top deck of the bus as we went through London. When we got to the restaurant, which was crowded but had several tables for two people still empty, the waiter immediately led us to a more spacious table for four. Above the table was a picture of animals, and my main power animal as well as my friend's were represented there (power animals are creatures who are our friends in our inner worlds, see Chapter 5, page 77 for more about them). Our Guides enhanced the fun and the synchronicity. When we came out of the restaurant to catch the bus home, we could feel ourselves being urged to get on the first bus that came. We thought it was not the right number and so continued to wait, especially as we could see what we thought was our bus immediately behind. Suddenly my friend and I both had the same sensation. Our Guides had left us and were merrily riding on the bus we had allowed to go! Imagine our chagrin when the driver of the bus that we thought was ours told us that at that time of night it was the bus that had just left that served our particular route and that the one we now wanted to take changed its route and did not go far enough for us. We had quite a cold wait for the next bus of the right number, but our Guides, having made a point, did return in order to keep us company and lighten our mood again.

Spirit Guides encourage us to live with celebration. They do not attempt to curb our sensuality, love of food, wine or conviviality. They do not require us to surround our lives with heavy disciplines in order to be able to communicate with them. They encourage us to take ourselves lightly and to be less self-judgemental. They teach that we learn from experience and that incarnate life can be a joy in every way. They encourage us to have a spiritual and symbolic viewpoint but also to be grounded and balanced. They often use the image of a tree, which grows tallest when its roots are most strong and secure in the earth. Spirituality is an embracing of life, not a separation of the earthly and the spiritual. Spirit resides in matter as well as in the more subtle worlds.

Do our Spirit Guides judge us and control us?

Spirit Guides never judge; they help us to learn from our experience and to grow strengths from our vulnerability. Far from wanting to control us they want us to enjoy the freedom of becoming our true or core selves, as I discuss in Chapter 4, page 48.

One of the obstacles to meeting your own Spirit Guide can be the desire to be controlled and directed. Many of us are wary of being controlled, but at the same time feel that it would be such a relief to have someone to tell us what to do in all situations or in the midst of each of life's challenges. Like adolescents we do not want to take full responsibility for our lives, but neither do we want to be curtailed in our freedoms. Spirit Guides are not there to be our parents but to be our friends and consultants and to show us true unconditional love. Occasionally they give categorical advice but never condemn us if we do not take it. They even stay around to help us 'pick up the pieces' when, by not listening to them, we have created havoc in our lives. They put us in touch with our own integrity and enable us to be self-determining and strong, but also feel supported and enjoy the benefit of their wisdom, experience and wider perspective.

If you want a Spirit Guide to make all your choices for you, then you are blocking your own quest, either for contact with your own Spirit Guide or for higher guidance from a channelled guide. If our Guides suspect that contact with them would mean that we hand them total power over our lives, then, for our own protection, they will be more elusive. I tend to think that one of my qualifications for having such a close contact with Gildas is that I am very stubborn and self-determining. There have been many times when lessons might have been easier if I had listened more, but I would have had far less respect for Gildas if he *had* tried to dictate all my choices. We need to grow towards a contemporary and mutually responsible relationship with our Spirit Guides and not be seeking parental care or our own special 'hotline to God', in order that their guidance can be true, higher guidance that speaks at a spiritual level to and from our souls.

Can I close the contact if I want to?

People do sometimes fear that if they make a connection with their Guides, life will never be the same again and they will not be able to 'go back', should they want to, to the way life was before. In some ways this is true, because once you have glimpsed these other worlds and felt the presence of your Spirit Guide, you can never really ever deny that dimension again. Hopefully, you would not want to. Is it not the same for every experience in life? Once we know something, we can't 'unknow' it, but we can decide whether or not we will use a learned skill. It is the same with learning to contact your Guide or other dimensions. Guides are such a joy to have alongside us in life, so gentle with our vulnerabilities and fears, so wise in the guidance they give us that it would be like a person with a broken leg refusing to wear a plaster or throwing away the walking stick too soon.

Since Spirit Guides do not seek to control us, they will not in any way force us to stay in contact with them. The connection is always ours to regulate. It is my belief, however, that our lives are guided by something beyond us even if we have never heard of Spirit Guides. We certainly don't have to hold them in our consciousness unless we want to, nor does having made a successful attempt to contact them commit us to continue that contact.

Guides never compromise our freedom to choose, including the freedom to choose whether we stay in conscious contact with them or not.

What are the dangers of false guidance?

False guidance is possible. There is no point in denying it. It is one of the reasons why I cannot stress too much that if you want to meet your Spirit Guide you will need to train yourself to reach the right level of awareness or consciousness. This is not difficult, and it has an inbuilt safety measure. All the exercises in this book are designed to take you to that level of awareness where it is no longer possible to meet lower or unevolved entities or any communicators from wherever they claim to come who are not on a true wisdom wavelength.

It is important to ask the right questions when seeking guidance (see Chapter 4, page 45). This is not only because it will enable the true Spirit Guides to help you most fully but also because the right questions attract the right kinds of communications and communicators.

Exercise 4, Chapter 4, page 60 and exercise 6, Chapter 5, page 84 go into more depth about self-protection, challenging or checking our otherworldly communicators and the use of allies in the inner and other worlds in order to keep you at the right level and 'on truth'.

When you seek guidance you must also keep your discernment faculties keen and aware. It is all too easy to be so 'glamoured' by the thought of contact with other worlds that normal access to critical judgement or assessment of what you are being told becomes clouded.

You are unlikely to be drawn into instances of false guidance if you bear in mind:

- that Guides don't know everything;
- that you need to reach the right level of awareness in order to contact true guidance;
- when receiving guidance from another channel you need to be reasonably assured that they, too, are attuned to a higher level of consciousness whilst channelling;
- that not every voice that purports to be speaking from other realms is necessarily wise.

It is possible to 'give your power away' when receiving guidance and to assume that if a Spirit Guide tells you to do something then that is exactly what you must do. Always be wary of Spirit Guides who give over-directive guidance. Most Guides will say: 'This is my perspective on your present dilemma; by giving it to you I hope I can give you reassurance and open some other choices for you – but the onus of choice always remains with you.' When we believe too strongly that there are absolutely right and absolutely wrong choices then we are vulnerable to over-directional guidance and too open to handing over our integrity and self-responsibility.

Amanda's story: false guidance
There are some lower entities on the other side, who, if they can 'get through', seem to enjoy any opportunity to direct or control people. On several occasions when people have been helped by Gildas through me, we have been asked to 'pick up some pieces' for those who have been victims of false guidance.

Amanda, whose life seemed directionless and full of losses of various kinds, had decided to ask for guidance from a friend who had suddenly developed an ability to channel. It was later realised that this friend had not looked deeply enough into the knowledge of what wise channelling might entail nor had she trained her own ability to sustain the right level of awareness. She was excited by the new ability she felt she had discovered and, without enough boundaries or structure to her attunement, just let what came to her pour forth.

At a time when her life was in turmoil, Amanda had been given guidance in an abrupt and authoritative style. In summary it said: 'You must get yourself to Australia as soon as you can. It is only there that you will find the new opportunities you seek. If you stay here your life will fall to pieces. Don't wait. Go as soon as possible. You will know what to do when you get there.'

Being desperate to bring change into her life, Amanda felt she had no choice but to do what was suggested. Without further thought, she packed everything up, said goodbye to friends and family and went to Australia with no clearly defined plans or objectives.

Amanda was depressed and confused, but the initial challenge of going so far away changed her mood to one of excitement and carried her on a wave of euphoria. She arranged to take an initial holiday period in Australia and hoped that the promise of 'you will know what to do when you get there' would be fulfilled and the way ahead for her would be clearly revealed. In fact she quickly discovered that she did not like Australia, its climate, or its way of life. She felt more lonely and defenceless than she had ever felt before and eventually came back feeling even more confused than when she went. She was trying to piece things together and understand what had happened and why her trust in the guidance she had received had been so misplaced, when she came, rather warily, to consult Gildas.

Although I think she had received false guidance and had been in an over-susceptible position when she had received her friend's channelling, Amanda's experience is also an example of there being no wrong decisions in life. The whole Australia episode had shaken and frightened her. In other ways, though, getting herself there had tested her resources. The courage required to go there alone had been considerable, as had been the courage needed once there, with many bridges seemingly burned behind her, to admit it was not the right move for her and to return to try, once again, to pick up the remnants of her life in England.

When Gildas pointed these things out to Amanda, she began to see that she was not a weak, gullible failure, but someone with the basic courage and determination to do what was necessary to build a new life. As she was directionless and without close family, Gildas gently suggested to her that perhaps there was some cause she could help or some service that she might get involved in, until she knew more clearly what she wanted to do with the rest of her life. After some consideration, Amanda applied to one of the schemes for over-seas volunteers and was accepted. She eventually fell in love with a co-volunteer and went to live, happily, in the United States. Although the initial guidance was false and of a style I would always consider suspect, and although Amanda and her friend, who was channelling with insufficient awareness, had much to learn about gullibility and discernment, the whole interaction nevertheless kick-started a chain of events that led Amanda to new fulfilment because she discovered her courage and inner resources. (See also colouring in guidance, Chapter 8, page 132.)

*   *   *

Now that we understand more about Spirit Guides and the enhancement they can bring to our lives, the next chapter gives specific advice and exercises for moving forward on our journey towards connection with them.

4

Preparing for Contact with our Spirit Guides

This chapter will help you attain the right 'mindset' before attempting the initial exercises that start you on the path to meeting your personal Spirit Guide. It ends with five core exercises to underpin your journey to guidance.

The first part of this book has been about Spirit Guides and issues relating to guidance. Now we turn to training and practicalities. The core exercises can set an exciting journey under way, but first of all you need to be clear about why you want to contact your Spirit Guide. Of course, you will have questions you want to ask of them, life issues you would like them to comment on and give you guidance about. Most Spirit Guides rely on the questions we ask in order to make a direct connection with us. But we need to be sure that our motives are clear and that any questions we ask are framed in a correct and clear way.

As we move to more specific training for meeting and working with our Spirit Guides we first of all need to remind ourselves that obtaining the most comprehensive and supportive answers from the other realms of being depends to a large extent upon having some understanding of the philosophies on which our Spirit Guides base their wisdom, as I discussed in Chapter 2. It is in this context that they deal with our questions, so if we remember this we are more likely to ask or phrase the kind of questions which will draw out the answers that most enhance our understanding.

If we want to be told exactly what to do and when to do it we are likely to be disappointed; if we ask: 'Will such and such happen and when will it happen?' we are likely to be disappointed; if we assume that we have no free will and that 'someone up there' is ordering our lives, we are likely to be disappointed. Not only will we be disappointed in the answers given by Spirit Guides we may consult through the various people who channel them, but also we may be disappointed with our own search for contact with our personal Spirit Guides and the guidance they give. Spirit Guides are not here to live our lives for us or to take all the challenges and dilemmas away. They will support us through the difficulties, they will help us with problem solving and with the ability to see a wider perspective, but the true Spirit Guides will rarely tell us categorically what to do.

When working with Gildas I do a lot of work by post or e-mail. This means that people I may never have met send me a list of questions accompanied by some background information about themselves and why they are asking these specific questions at this specific time. In contrast, when people come to consult us in person, I also ask them to prepare their questions, but usually, if it is a first session of guidance for them, I discuss these with them before tuning in to Gildas. In this preliminary look at the questions, I may encourage the client to modify them a little, open them out more or phrase them in a wider sense.

Gildas does not, and will not, work clairvoyantly. Although he does not condemn clairvoyance as such, when we are on a serious spiritual quest, he doesn't feel that seeing or knowing the future in a clairvoyant way is always as helpful as we might be tempted to believe. Therefore, he asks for some personal background information. In giving responses and information, whether the client is present or not, Gildas is able to look at subtle energy lines and patterns around the client that give him a wider spiritual and evolutionary perspective. He often says that he does not have many direct answers to personal questions, only commentary around the dilemmas from which the questions have arisen. He looks at auras and chakras (our personal energy centres) and sees past-life themes (although rarely the minute details) that may have a bearing on the present quandary. Through these perspectives, he encourages everything to be viewed in a wider framework. He aims to minimise guilt and self-blame and also to encourage people to give themselves permission to do what they know they *want* to do in a given situation, as distinct from being over-influenced into 'oughts' and 'shoulds' because of conditioning and/or the emotional pleas and needs of others.

Some people don't want to give details or even to ask questions; they long to be just 'seen' or 'read' and told what to do. The following type of questions usually receive unsatisfactory answers or our Spirit Guides have to explain why definitive answers cannot be given and that life does not necessarily come with a route map:

- 'Will I meet my soul mate and be together with them, and when will that happen?'
- 'Will we have children, and how many?'
- 'Where should I live?'
- 'When should I move?'
- 'Am I in the right country?'
- 'Where is my mother/father/brother/sister that I lost contact with?'
- 'What is my purpose in life?'
- 'What career should I follow?'
- 'Should I/Am I meant to emigrate to America?'

On the other hand, the same questions phrased differently might elicit helpful information, teaching or support:

- 'Is it likely that I will meet my soul mate?'
- 'Can you see any reason why I should not have a successful partnership in this lifetime?'
- 'Can you help me to see what I am learning from having spent

so many years of this lifetime without partnership, and is there anything I can do that might change that?'

- 'Can you see any reason why I should not have children in this lifetime?'

- 'Is it a valid choice for me to want to be alone in this lifetime/at this phase of my life?'

- 'Given my life history and what you might be able to see of my soul contract, can you point me in any direction I could follow that might bring me more satisfaction than another?'

- 'I am thinking of emigrating to America, can you tell me what might be positive and what might be negative about this?'

- 'Is there any geographical area that might suit my particular energies better than the area I am living in now?'

In some ways the questions are the same, but whereas the first set assumes that one way may be right and another wrong, or that we have no choice in life decisions, the second set asks for information or a wider perspective against which to make choices. The Guide being consulted is invited to interpret some of the purposes the soul or higher self might have had in setting the individual certain challenges and tests.

The true, or core self

In his responses to people, whether concerning spiritual growth or when making life decisions, Gildas often refers to the need to cultivate, know and be faithful to one's 'true self' – sometimes referred to as the 'core self' (see Anthony's story, Chapter 1, page 15).

One of the best ways in which to prepare to meet our Spirit Guides is to work at becoming our true selves. This involves knowing and understanding the influences that have shaped and conditioned us so that we can decide which of these are harmonious for us and need to be built on, and those which in some way may be stifling us and need to be left behind (see exercise 8, Chapter 8 page 137).

This true self is not the same as soul, or spirit or higher self. It is best described as our psychological true self. In each personality, in each lifetime, there is a potential or blueprint in us. With upbringing and the challenges of life, we may lose the way to the true self or in some way lose permission to be who we really are. Conformity to certain images or ways of being is very strongly underlined in the society of today. People with originality of expression and idea are too easily labelled 'eccentric', 'way out' or a 'dropout'.

A gardener who decides to plant some unlabelled but interesting-looking seeds will watch their growth carefully, assessing their needs as they grow. He will be interested to observe their progress and see what sort of plant each is becoming. Should there be a flower or fruit, he will be delighted with the result. Whatever the shape, colour or size, he will be pleased if each plant is healthy and flourishing. He will let those that want to grow tall have support; he will see that the shorter, bushier ones have enough light and ground space.

A gardener knows that a seed contains a certain blueprint or potential. It is useless to plant a tomato seed if you want to grow an oak tree; no amount of persuasion, tending, discipline or threat will make the seed change what it is able to produce. Also, if the conditions are not right for the seed, it will sicken and die.

Of course, the analogy between a seed and a human being cannot be pushed too far, but nevertheless it serves to set us thinking about our nature and true purpose. However much we may struggle to gain approval or to be what others ask of us, our feelings and emotions will eventually make it clear if we have become 'a square peg in a round hole'.

If feelings are ignored and the mind pushes us on, or entrenches us further in areas where we cannot express the true self, the body will begin to collude. It will become the servant of our emotions, because when the body fails, life change may be forced upon us. When we learn to listen to our emotions and our bodies, endeavouring to understand the messages we are being given, we may be able to choose change before change chooses us.

As we can see from the two case histories in Chapter 1, it is not easy to make decisions when divided loyalties are part of the picture. There is sometimes an exceedingly fine line between being self-indulgent, complacent and serving our own needs without any reference to the needs of others and making choices that give ourselves *and* others the space we require. Sacrificing our visions can lead to resentments and depression. Feeling that we are letting others down can be very uncomfortable indeed. Usually, miraculously, if we consider our true selves in the right way, creative compromises happen or are made. The two personal stories in Chapter 1 illustrate this to some extent.

If we work to know and fulfil our true selves, we usually become healthy and vital in every way and on every level. When asked questions about purpose in life, Gildas often answers that we all have a common purpose, which is to find our true selves and that this *is* also our soul purpose. What we are usually meaning when we ask about purpose is more to do with 'How can I serve?', but usually the best way to serve humanity is to live from our true, innate integrity, to get clear of conditioning and cease to model ourselves too closely on what others want or expect. If you are an apple tree, don't try to be a peach, be the best apple tree you possibly can – and vice versa.

Your Spirit Guide will be more than ready to help you on the path to becoming your true self, and the progress you make in this way will not only strengthen the integrity of your personal contact with your Guide but will also mean that if you eventually decide to channel for others you will be less likely to 'colour' your channelling negatively (see Chapter 8, page 130).

When you meet your Spirit Guide the best questions to ask will usually be connected with getting your Guide to talk to you about his or her philosophy of evolution. Although I have found that most Guides work from the sort of philosophical basis I have outlined in Chapter 2, you will also need to ask your personal Spirit Guide for their particular perspective on this so that you can understand the purpose they are serving in seeking to be heard. Spirit Guides are usually as eager for contact with us as we are for contact with them.

Through us the Guides fulfil part of their purposes of service to humanity and evolution.

Another area of questioning for your Guide is to ask for help in training yourself to be as clear a channel as possible and to receive guidance and support coherently and unambiguously (see also Chapter 8, page 130).

Open expectation

It is important to have an open rather than a specific expectation when preparing to meet our Spirit Guides. If we work towards having a greater consciousness of our Guides, they will respond to our invitation and endeavour. If, however, as we strive to build the bridge of communication, we become too fixed on a particular expectation of how guidance is received, including what we shall see or hear, the ways in which we will receive information and even the kind of information we expect to have access to, then we may inadvertently block or undervalue the unique and perhaps subtle ways in which our individual guidance will manifest itself.

Having open expectations means we are less likely to try and receive guidance in the way we think it *ought* to be received. Being 'open' in this way is also likely to sharpen our perceptions. In channelling workshops, I always emphasise that although I am willing to demonstrate how I receive communication from Gildas, the demonstration is in no way intended to be a model of what 'should' happen. One of the joys of meeting our Guides and learning to be closer to them and their communication is the individuality of the experience and the creativity in each and every contact.

Inner wisdom

Our desire to get a clear vision of a magnificent Guide in full Native American regalia, in Egyptian or Atlantean garb, or a gentle, blue-robed Sister of Mercy, is understandable. Such clarity makes us feel that we are getting 'results' and we may consider it to be reassuring or evidential. Never rule out the idea that this *could* happen to you, but don't *expect* it to be so. The first nuances of guidance are usually much more subtle.

Within each one of us there is a source of inner wisdom. When we learn to contact that inner wisdom first and to take it with us on our search or endeavour to meet our Spirit Guides, then we are more likely to be able to perceive what we *do* receive and be able to know how to build the bridge of communication, strand by strand, until it is fully open to us whenever we want it.

Inner wisdom and centring into it can be as simple as quietly and meditatively focusing ourselves, so that we know we are in a place where the aspects of life and questions we are asking ourselves and others are no longer 'pulling' at us. Most of us will have experience of such a place and know that even if we can access it for only a few moments, we will gain a sense of calm and fresh perspective. If we have been in a quandary about something and we are able to centre into such a place, we can sometimes find, as we return to everyday life again, that almost miraculously the answer to the quandary is known to us or the problem is no longer so pressing, or even no longer exists.

Finding this quiet point of centring can be an inner meditative process and below I give an exercise for finding such an inner point. For some of us, it may be that we need to go and look at or touch a favourite tree, or plant or flower, to watch water flowing, to listen to some music, read some poetry or even have a fragrant bath or shower so that we can find this quiet point. The state of centring does not depend on an ability to meditate, but it does depend on knowing what will quieten and relax us and put us in a place of peace – and then remembering, in the midst of a stressful day or predicament, to make it happen.

The act of centring, then, places us in touch with something that puts problems into proportion or may even resolve them for us. As we begin the journey to connect with Spirit Guides, it is also good to learn about our inner world or landscape and to use that interior ground as preparation for finding the right level of consciousness so that we can most successfully and safely meet them. I include here a second meditation exercise, which is about consciously entering your inner landscape and perhaps meeting with a figure or an essence that represents your inner wisdom – the part of you that knows – another aspect of the still, calm point, beyond the tumult of outer life. Your inner wise being or presence is not a Spirit Guide, but an inner personification of wisdom and balance. Having access to this presence, as Guide companion, protector and ally, can be useful in journeying to meet your discarnate Spirit Guide from the other realms of being.

Preparing for the exercises

Before beginning the following exercises may I remind you that it is a good idea to read through the whole book before you begin the journey proper.

Once you begin, try to do the exercises regularly but not to an over-assiduous discipline. You will soon find which exercises are most helpful to your needs and you can then design a development programme for yourself, using them as a basis. Exercise 1 is the only one that I would say you might consider using daily or even more than once a day. It is invaluable in helping you to stay grounded and in touch with everyday life whilst building the facility to be at home in other worlds or dimensions.

Some people find it a good idea to record the exercises, so that you can listen to the instructions as you go, rather than having to remember a sometimes complex sequence.

The exercises in the book are numbered from 1 to 11 and this is the sequence that I recommend you follow, at least initially. Later you may choose to leave some out and focus more on others, but the higher the number of the exercise the more pre-knowledge or experience it assumes. The earlier exercises help you to build on that knowledge and experience sequentially.

It makes sense to do these exercises at times when you know you are most likely to be undisturbed. Unplug the phone, plan to ignore the doorbell and make sure that your children or your partner are either out or realise and respect that you need peace and privacy for a while.

Some people lose body heat when they go into a slightly altered state of awareness, so have a blanket or a wrap near you for warmth and comfort if you should need it.

It is easy to assume that you need to sit in a lotus or classic meditation posture in order to get the best out of these journeys and techniques. This is not necessarily so. It is important to be comfortable and for your body to be supported where and when it needs support. Sitting with your feet in touch with the ground helps grounding and polarity, but unless lying down automatically signals sleep for you, there is no reason why you should not lie on a bed, a couch or on the floor. Create a quiet space for yourself and take up a position that you find comfortable. Sit in a cross-legged or lotus position on a chair or the floor if you wish, but if you are sitting in an upright chair or lying down, do not cross your legs at the ankles or knees and do not fold or cross your arms. Have your hands relaxed and your palms and fingers open but forming a cup-like shape. Find the position that most helps you to be relaxed and which enables your creativity to flow.

Once you decide to make the journey to contact your Spirit Guide with serious intention, it is good to provide yourself with a special book in which you can record the exercises you do and the results they bring. Be creative with this. It is a good idea to give it a title such as: 'My Journey to Guidance', 'My Spirit Guide Book', 'My Spirit Guide Journal', or something that reflects your intent to develop this special connection. Always have crayons or pastels or even paints to hand, so that you can make an imaginative record of your experiences. Dating each entry can be of help in assessing your progress.

Exercise 1 should always be performed before any other exercise, to help your preparation and balance. At the end of each exercise I always suggest that you put a 'cloak of light with a hood' right around you and that you be aware of your feet in contact with the ground. This means that if you are lying down, it is a good idea to sit up for this ending ritual and to put your feet on the ground. The cloak of light helps to close down any subtle centres you may have opened; it means that you take light with you wherever you go, but also that the light protects and contains you and helps your transition from one state of awareness to another.

Exercise 1: Grounding and 'running energy'

Parallel to our physical spine there is a central column of subtle energy. To maintain balance, groundedness and good energetic health, energy should run freely through this column in two directions. Imagining, breathing and visualising this energy flow help it to be vital. I give here two versions of this basic exercise, which is useful for general relaxation and revitalisation as well as for preparation for all spiritual work. Both versions are breathing exercises, but the second has visualisation with it, for those who prefer the visual approach.

Non-visual method
1. Begin by being aware of the rhythm of your breathing and letting it slow down a little.

2. Now draw the breath in as though it comes from just above the crown of your head: draw it down through the centre of your body, just in front of your spine; change to the out-breath at a point that feels natural for you, which will probably be around your solar plexus area (the central point just above your waist), but may be higher or lower. Keep breathing downwards on the out-breath as though right down through your legs and into the earth. If you are sitting in a cross-legged or lotus position, the breath will not go down through your legs but straight out through your perineum area and into the earth. Breathe in this way for about five breath sequences (one in/out breath equals one breath sequence).

3. Now, having breathed the fifth breath sequence out into the earth, begin to alternate the breath sequence, so that you breathe up from the earth, through the centre of your body, changing to the out-breath at a point that is comfortable for you, continuing to breathe upwards on the out-breath and letting it finally go up and out through the crown of your head. The next breath sequence will be as the first five breath sequences but the following one will be from earth to crown again, establishing a rhythm of alternating up/down breaths.

4. Continue to breathe in this way, without straining, for no more than five minutes. Always end on the downward breath sequence, repeating it in this direction more than once if you wish, as you finish.

Visual method

If you like visualisation, or want to vary the exercise, here is a visual version. If the outside conditions are favourable and there is a suitable tree that you know, it can be good to do this exercise in a standing position with your back against the tree and your bare feet on the earth. At other times follow the posture instructions given in this chapter on page 54.

1. Begin by being aware of your breathing rhythm; allow it to become steady and slow down a little.

2. Visualise yourself as a tree: your branches stretch out above; your roots stretch deeply down into the earth; your trunk is straight and strong. You are nurtured by the four elements: sun (fire) warms you and air refreshes you, your roots are firmly in the earth and they seek the underground streams and sources of living water.

3. Breathe in through your branches, from the elements of air and sun, take the breath right down through your trunk and breathe out strongly into your roots, into the earth and the streams of living water.

4. Breathe in now from the earth and the living water, bring the breath up through your roots, through your trunk, into your branches and breathe out into the elements of air and sun.

5. Repeat these two breath sequences for no longer than five minutes. Gradually let the visualisation fade. Feel your feet firmly on the ground, your own space all around you and proceed with a sense of centredness to practise your chosen exercise.

You are now ready for any exercise for connecting with Spirit Guidance that you have chosen to work with, although working gradually through them all in sequence at least once is recommended, especially if you are completely new to this kind of work.

Exercise 2: *Finding the place of inner peace and wisdom*

You can use this exercise at any time that you want to feel centred or in touch with your own inner peace and wisdom. Use it as an extra preparation for other exercises, or in order to help you get a new 'take' on everyday problems and dilemmas.

1. Be in touch with the rhythm of your breathing. Do not try to alter or force your breath, just follow each in-breath and each out-breath until you begin to feel centred, calm, relaxed and peaceful.

2. Now visualise or sense your heart centre or chakra – the energy centre in the centre of your body, near your physical heart. Visualise it opening up like a rose opens with the sun, from its closed but loose bud, to a full rose in perfect bloom. Imagine a pink rose, with a beautiful fragrance and, as it opens, you see that at its centre there is a touch of gold.

3. Focus your attention on to the gold centre, and feel as though you are sitting or lying surrounded by a gently fragrant golden light, which is the still point of your being, the place where you sense wisdom and knowing.

4. Remain in this centre, quiet and at peace but also alert, for up to ten minutes, knowing that when you return to your everyday world you may have gained a new perspective on any pressing problems or worries that have been besetting you.

5. When you are ready, return to an awareness of the rhythm of your breathing. Let the petals of the rose at your heart centre gently close in, not shutting that centre down or off, but protecting the inner golden place.

6. Feel the contact with the ground beneath your feet. Take your sense of peace with you as you resume your normal life once more.

Exercise 3: Guided journey to contact your inner wise being or presence

Within us all there is an inner landscape, which is full of places of inspiration and inner aspects that we can learn to meet at will.

These inner aspects are not Spirit Guides but are personified inner resources. One of those, which it is valuable to sense or meet early on in any pathway towards meeting with a Spirit Guide, is the sense or being of an inner wise presence. You may know little about your inner worlds and their resources, but if you trust the process, it will usually be there when you call for it. Your inner wise presence may be sensed as energy, seen as a colour or met as a being. As long as you are open to sensing as well as seeing, when you call for a wise presence to be with you it is almost certain that you will feel accompanied and blessed in some way. You will particularly benefit from this exercise when you have read the whole of this book, before you begin your development programme in earnest.

1. Become aware of the rhythm of your breathing and bring that rhythm into your heart centre or chakra, thus activating your heart energy with which you can travel into your inner landscape. Find yourself in a meadow and take the opportunity to activate all your inner senses so that you see the objects and colours, hear the sounds, touch the textures, smell the fragrances and savour the tastes.

2. Be aware of your inner landscape around and beyond your meadow. Know that somewhere in this landscape your inner wise presence dwells. You can either journey to that dwelling place, for a part of you knows well how to find the pathway, or you can call your wise presence towards you now, to meet you in your meadow.

3. At your journey's goal, or whenever you call your wise presence, you may experience an atmosphere of wise understanding, or you may see colours, hear a beautiful sound, smell a special fragrance or meet a being. As you either experience this presence or see your inner wise being,

ask for a blessing on your inner life and your search for connection with your Spirit Guide.

4. You may receive a special gift or talisman for use in this work, or be given a keyword, feel a lightening of your heart or the knowledge that you are guided and protected. If you receive none of these, then know that there will be other opportunities to meet your wise presence and that this journey has been important in paving the way.

5. Spend up to ten minutes enjoying the company of your inner wise presence and then, if you have journeyed beyond it, return to your meadow and then to the rhythm of your breathing in your heart centre. Become aware of your body, your contact with the ground and your normal surroundings.

6. Imagine that there is a cloak of light with a hood right around you and be aware of your feet in contact with the ground.

7. Give yourself the opportunity to record this journey in your special book.

Exercise 4: Asking three main questions

This exercise covers several aspects that are important when seeking closer contact with your personal Spirit Guide. It also helps to differentiate the way you *think* about things and the way you *feel* about things, so that you come to a greater clarity about any blockages that may be standing in your way or taking energy and attention from the business of moving forward in both your outer life and your inner, or spiritual, life.

I use this exercise on a regular basis to help get myself into the right frame of mind for receiving guidance and to check whether any conditioning or mental expectations of myself may be blocking my feelings or emotions, or vice versa.

Below, I give the exercise in its entirety, but you will see that it has several stages or sections. You may want to take sufficient time to consider all these stages in one long session of self-reflection or you may want to spread each stage over several days or parts of a day.

It can be helpful to get a partner or good friend to do this exercise as well, either together or separately, but with the aim of being able to discuss and compare each other's responses and reactions later.

1. Before you begin, have some large sheets of paper and some coloured crayons or pens to hand. The exercise requires at least three sheets of paper, but have at least another three sheets in reserve, as you may need more.

2. Prepare one sheet of paper for each of the questions this exercise covers by writing each question as a heading on its own separate sheet: 'Where am I now?', 'What are my guidance needs?' and 'What question(s) should I be asking now?' One side of each sheet of paper is to be used for jotting down your immediate answers to, or thoughts on, each of these questions.

3. When you are sure that you will be undisturbed and have created a quiet space around you, take a pen or pencil and the first sheet of paper headed 'Where am I now?' and begin to think about your life as it is now, including a review of what has led you to be where you are now, thoughts on how you want to change or develop your life situation and any obstacles you see as hindering changes you want to make. Be honest and practical as you write this mini-review of your life and the circumstances and situation in which you find yourself now. If you want to take a break and return to this

task in order to add more or revise what you have already written, then do so.

4. When you are ready, take the next sheet of paper headed: 'What are my guidance needs?' This question requires taking into consideration the things you have written on your first sheet of paper and reflecting on the areas where you may need practical or outer guidance, help or support, and the people or resources you might be able to consult. List the things that you may need to gather more practical information about in order to be able to consider realistically the current scope or possibilities for making certain types of change or resolving a present dilemma.

5. When you have reflected on these practical needs, also reflect on whether you need guidance to put things into a wider context. Ask yourself whether this is a time when you perhaps need the kind of overview of your life and the potential or consequences of choices you might now be considering that a Spirit Guide could give.

6. As and when you feel ready, take your third sheet of paper, headed: 'What question(s) should I be asking now?' Review what you have written on your previous sheets of paper and get a sense of how to word questions about any issues that are now coming to the fore for you.

7. Finally, see whether you can make one, but not more than three, succinct questions that you really need to be pondering now. Try to make your questions as open-ended as possible, so rather than: 'Do I need to move house?', you might ask: 'What might be the advantages to my moving house at this time in my life?' and, rather than: 'What job/work should I be doing now?', you could ask: 'Would a

change of lifestyle help me to have more sense of purpose?'
Most importantly try to avoid questions that begin: 'Am I
meant to be/do/have'.

8. Your written and cognitive answers to the questions around
   which this exercise is formed should now be on one side of
   each of your large sheets of paper, so that you can turn to the
   blank sides as you prepare for the next stage. If you have
   written very freely and already turned the page, you will need
   to bring your reserve paper into use. It is important now to
   have a blank sheet in front of you. You will also, for this section
   of the exercise, need your coloured pens, crayons or pastels
   and, for clarity, you may like to write each question again on
   the blank sides or fresh sheets of your paper.

The next part of the exercise is meditative, so follow the general
preparation instructions given on page 53.

1. Become aware of the rhythm of your breathing. Gradually
   allow each in-breath and out-breath to help the focus of your
   attention come into your heart centre or chakra, which is in
   the centre of your body on the same level as your physical
   heart. As you breathe in and out with this focus, you will be
   activating your heart energy, which helps inner wisdom,
   creativity and intuition to flow.

2. In your heart energy hold the question: 'Where am I now?'
   and seek as a response an image or symbol. When you have
   one, express and develop it by beginning to draw
   meditatively on your paper. If no image or symbol comes
   easily, after a while start to draw anyway, meditatively,
   intuitively and creatively without self-judgement, even if it
   seems as though you are only 'playing' with the colours.

3. When you have finished this method of response to the first question, take a short break or decide to do this part of the exercise with the next questions later. Whatever gap you decide to leave between each question, repeat the procedure above with: 'What are my guidance needs?' and 'What question(s) should I be asking now?'

4. When you have all your material from each part of this exercise you can reflect on all that you have written and drawn and, if possible, share it with a partner or good friend. Don't try in any way to 'analyse' your drawings, but get a sense as to whether they are in harmony with what you have written or whether they bring in something from your feeling, intuitive and creative side that either enhances what you have thought and written or puts a different perspective on it.

Having completed this exercise you now have a question or questions that can be used in the pattern of your journey to connection with guidance and your Spirit Guide. You may also already have some sense of the wider or deeper issues you are encountering as you seek to move forward in your life now. You are ready to move on now to exercise 5, below.

Exercise 5: Journeying to the right level of awareness

If you learn to travel to a slightly altered state of consciousness and to build the bridge of connection with your Spirit Guide on a vibration that touches into the higher planes of being and awareness, then you will be able to meet your Guide safely and without any fear of interference from lower entities (see Chapter 5, page 76 for more on lower entities).

This guided journey to a meeting place holds the symbolism that enables you to reach the right level of awareness. It is a symbolic journey, but because in your inner landscape you journey upwards to a plateau near the top of a mountain, you will also journey within yourself to a meeting place that is at, but not above, the level of consciousness you need to reach. This level can also be reached by focusing on certain chakras, and I have included a brief introduction to them and another version of this exercise that uses the chakras in exercise 7, Chapter 7, page 122. (See also Further Reading, my book *Working with your Chakras*.)

This exercise is for building a bridge towards guidance – the rainbow bridge, which forms a structure for our Spirit Guides to cross. If you are new to this work, I do advise you to read right through this book before inviting a Guide or presence to come to you on the plateau or at the entrance to the rainbow bridge. Read, especially, the advice given in Chapter 5, page 76 before you do this exercise. If a Guide does appear and you feel comfortable and ready, follow the advice given there, or put a cloak of light with a hood right around you and return to your meadow. Then, through becoming aware of your body and your breath in your heart centre, return to your everyday level of awareness.

When you are ready to practise this exercise, make the preparations described on page 54 and refer to exercise 1, page 55 and exercise 2, page 57, as they are now incorporated into this longer, fuller journey.

1. Become aware of the rhythm of your breathing. Gradually bring that rhythm into your heart centre or chakra and recreate your place of inner wisdom (exercise 1, page 55).

2. Travel, using your heart and wisdom energy, into your inner landscape, and find yourself in a meadow. Activate all your inner senses so that you see the objects and colours, smell the fragrances, hear the sounds, touch the textures and savour

the tastes. Call to your inner wise being or presence to accompany you on this next stage of your journey (exercise 2, page 57).

3. From your meadow, look out at the surrounding landscape. Nearby, there is a winding pathway that leads into a hilly area and you can see that it continues up into some mountains. The pathway leads to a plateau that is near the top of one of the mountains. As you look ahead you see that this plateau seems to be particularly alive and full of light, so that you feel very happy to be journeying there.

4. Call your inner wise presence or being to join you in your meadow and to be alongside you as you make this extended journey into the area of your inner landscape (exercise 2, page 57).

5. Follow your pathway to the plateau in your own time, looking at the landscape as you go, noting all the features you see and the panorama you get as you go higher.

6. The path winds and the journey is surprisingly easy. Gradually you are going upwards, but you can always see your meadow below and the attractive plateau ahead.

7. When you reach the plateau, take time to explore. You will probably find a source of clear, running, living water from which to refresh yourself, and there may be a small sanctuary or travellers' rest for you to enter and explore. There will also be a place of natural sanctuary, with a sun-warmed rock against which to rest your back and look out over the landscape and, magically, there is a place where a rainbow light shines. This is like the place of fairytales, where the rainbow meets the earth and bridges out beyond.

8. This is the meeting place which you can, eventually, step into and invite your Spirit Guide to come across the rainbow bridge to meet you.

9. On this occasion be content to see this place where the rainbow bridge runs between your inner landscape and other planes and spheres. Do not step into the rainbow, or invite your Spirit Guide, as yet, to join you here. Instead, find a place where you are happy to sit and wait, with an open heart and an open expectation. If you have any questions that have arisen from exercise 3, page 58, you might hold these in your heart energy and heart breath, pondering them in a relaxed way, and knowing that your inner wise being or presence is with you.

10. Know that at this place you have made your part of the journey. This territory is yours, part of your inner landscape, but be aware that particularly in the rainbow area it is a bridge to other worlds and other spheres.

11. Remain in your chosen comfortable place for no more than ten minutes. When you are ready to return, refresh yourself once more from the source of living water. Know that having found and established this place in your inner landscape you can always return to it, but now make your way back to the meadow, from which all these journeys begin and in which all these journeys end.

12. From the meadow, return to awareness of your breath in your heart centre and so to the awareness of your breath in your body. Become conscious of the whole of your body and where you are sitting in your normal, everyday world. Feel your contact with the ground, open your eyes and connect with your outer surroundings, before closing them again and

putting a cloak of light with a hood right around you and being aware of your feet in contact with the ground.

13. Before you return to your everyday routines take the time to record this journey in your special book.

In this chapter we have moved on to preparatory exercises to start the exciting journey to contact our Spirit Guides. In Chapter 5 the journey continues with more practical guidance and the next exercises that will help to make the vision into the reality.

5

Moving on from your Basic Work

Each person will react differently to the basic work practised in exercises 1–5 and will also experience different results from them. These initial exercises help you to become familiar with your inner territory and with the rainbow bridge meeting place. However, the final stages of the basic journey to guidance have not yet been added. This chapter will look at other questions you may have about the journey. There are also other things apart from formal exercises and guided journeys that you can do to expedite meeting your Spirit Guide, and the aim now is to show ways in which the relationship or your openness to it can be built.

Often, at this stage people begin to wonder how they can recognise the difference between the various levels or potential sources of communication. How do you know whether any guidance you receive is coming from your inner wise presence, your Spirit Guide, higher self or guardian angel? How do you keep safe in your inner worlds and at the interface with other worlds? Do you need to challenge any guidance presence you sense? As you read on, I hope your horizons will be broadened and that any questions you may have will be answered. Remember that I have used these exercises and methods, combined with this detailed information, with many people, both in one-to-one situations and workshops. The process has its own way of unfolding for each individual, and if you persevere by following the basic guidelines and structures you will find that awareness of guidance in your life and eventually contact with your own personal Spirit Guide will result, as well as gaining the ability to differentiate between different levels of experience.

Some of you will find visualisation more difficult than others. Try not to be put off by this but take heart from Melanie's story on page 82 and understand that subtle perceptive skills can be developed or different ways of entry to the inner worlds can be found.

Building the relationship

A good way to build the relationship with your Spirit Guide is to 'act as if'. This means that although you may not yet have had direct experience of your Guide, you begin to increase your focus on asking for guardianship, help or inspiration.

To a large extent our personal Spirit Guides see and know about many of the circumstances and details of our personal lives, but we should never assume that there is, therefore, no need to communicate our thoughts and feelings to them. A Guide is a friend, and when we have a good friend or partner we share our views, perceptions and emotions with them. We need to do the same with our Guides.

You may already be in the habit of keeping a journal. From the moment that you decide you want to train yourself to have more connection with your Spirit Guide, you should address your journal – either your regular journal or another one, such as the special book you keep for guidance work – to your Guide, as I discussed in Chapter 4, page 54). As you write, or draw, imagine that this discarnate being or energy is beside you, attending with empathy and wisdom to the entries you make in your book. Perhaps you will sense some words or thoughts of comfort, or you may suddenly see a new angle on an aspect of your life. As this happens, note it down as a possible communication from your Spirit Guide or from your inner wisdom source.

Make a habit of lighting a candle or nightlight at least once a day. As you light and dedicate this candle, include a request to your

Guide to be alongside you in the energy of the candlelight, and ask, as part of your dedication or candle-lighting focus, that contact with your Spirit Guide may be strengthened and furthered. (Remember, never to leave a lighted candle unattended.)

It is good, too, to get into the habit of sitting with a lighted candle for an extended period of reflection, meditation or contemplation. Have a notebook and/or a tape recorder on hand and simply enter into a quiet, focusing and inner-listening mode. Perhaps there will be an issue about your life in your mind, and, as you sit, you may become aware of images or new clarifying thoughts about this issue. Draw them, write them down or dictate what you are receiving into a tape recorder. You may eventually recognise that at least some of this communication and support is coming from your Spirit Guide.

Get used to drawing what you are seeing, as you are seeing it, writing down or recording on tape coherent thoughts or messages as you access them. This will help you to find the modes in which you most easily receive communication from your Spirit Guide or inner wisdom. At first you may use a variety of modes, but gradually you will find the one that is most comfortable for you and feels easiest to use as your method of channelling messages from your Spirit Guide and the other realms of being.

How do I know who is giving me guidance?

This is a question you are bound to ask at this stage. As you sense that you are receiving some communication through thoughts, feelings, inner knowing and even coherent subtle messages, it is natural that you will feel the need to understand how this is happening or differentiate who may be in touch with you from inner or outer realms.

However frustrating it may seem in the early stages of training yourself to receive guidance, it is best not to try too hard with this one. Rather than focusing on identifying the specific source, concentrate on the quality and tone of what you receive: if it helps, if it comes with an atmosphere of love and care and you feel gently touched by its wisdom, comfort and understanding, that is all that need concern you until you have built up more experience.

As the experience builds up, so you will find yourself recognising the source of each aspect of your guidance, almost without knowing how you are doing it. The differences between the places or communicators from which guidance comes are extremely subtle. Any communication within your inner landscape or from a Guide you meet at the rainbow bridge may be perceived as fragrance, colour, a difference in wavelength or vibration, or as a sense of resonance coming from a consistent direction. Your inner wise presence might communicate from your heart centre area, in words, inferences or colours; your higher self might give you a sense of inner knowing or realisation; your Spirit Guide might give you symbols or clear words; your guardian angel might touch you subtly with his or her wings or give you words that feel as if they are a clear bell note, which is usually a higher tone than any felt or subtly heard note from a Spirit Guide. At first you will not know which is which, but gradually you will realise that there is a consistency of one sort or another; you will begin to know which source is which, or you will be content simply to receive that which you differentiate as wisdom from another perspective without worrying about its exact source.

Gildas is never far away from me, and I experience his essence, energy, colour, vibration and fragrance. By subtle changes in my perception of these, I know when he is ready to communicate and when I am sufficiently attuned for him to be able to do so. I perceive him as being alongside me in the area of my left shoulder, and the words he imprints into my awareness come in through my left ear, although not as actual sounds.

I sense my female Guide, who I rarely channel publicly, as facing me and surrounding me with a cloak of gentleness; she has a subtle sound around her, like running water.

The inner knowing that I associate with my inner wise presence comes from within me at my heart level. It is a heart-felt recognition and knowing.

Communications from my higher self are usually accompanied by a vivid violet, mauve or gold colour and I can sense a 'line' of connection coming in from above the crown of my head and activating my brow, throat and heart chakras (see Chapter 7 for more about chakras).

Angelic communications are usually sensed on a very light note, approaching at an angle, from above, behind or either side. I experience a subtle, warming light. These communications are usually short, often just giving a moment of vision or comfort. Where words come, they are like a gentle tinkling and don't have the deeper resonance of sustained communication that I sense when in contact with Gildas.

I can write about these differences relatively clearly now, but I have only been able to know them through experience, and this is the only way to obtain clarity of recognition. You need to persist and subtly observe, knowing that the distinction and the certainty will gradually come.

Your inner landscape and inner senses

At this point, it seems appropriate to include a note about your inner landscape and inner sensing or senses. We all have an inner world. You may know this already as a landscape, a place of daydreams or fantasy that is yours to use for comfort, inner play or creativity, or it may be that you do not find inner picturing and the concept of an inner landscape to be as easy or natural as this.

Your inner world, however, may be more one of mental dialogue. There are few people who do not find themselves having inner discussions of one kind or another. We often say, when faced with a choice: 'Well part of me wants this, and part wants that.' Most of us will relate to the concept of 'giving myself a good talking to'. Such phrases are part of the phenomenon we all eventually recognise. We are complex beings and can have many aspects or voices arising from within us. The concept of the 'inner wise being or presence' (as I discussed in exercise 3, Chapter 4, page 58) is of a voice or presence within each one of us that gathers together all our integrity and our experience of life; it takes a certain distance or detachment, adds a measure of creativity and so puts us in touch with a place of personal inner truth and authority from which clarity can come.

These different parts of ourselves, whether we sense them as voices or thoughts or whether we find them easy to picture as identities with whom we can converse, are known in the world of transpersonal psychology as subpersonalities. These distinct universes within us provide richness and an inner dimension. They arise as survival mechanisms from the results of upbringing and conditioning. Bringing them into a greater, conscious recognition can help us in our search for the psychological transparency that helps to make us clear channels for Spirit Guides as I will discuss in Chapter 8.

Our subpersonalities inhabit our inner worlds, thus making knowledge of inner worlds an even more valuable tool as we take the journey of self-growth. These inner worlds or landscapes also hold symbolic resources, such as places of healing and rest, inner temples of being, the river of life, the tree of life, the inner cave and the inner fire, to name but a few. In the inner landscape, too, we find the places where our power animals and other inner allies, such as the inner healer, inner alchemist or inner parent, reside.

Our inner landscape holds a balance of the four elements, earth, air, fire and water, and when we travel in our inner worlds we can activate our inner senses, so that we see, hear, taste, feel and smell what we are experiencing. Inner sensing comes naturally to some of us but not to all. As you start the guidance quest, at first it is common to find it difficult to be able to use the richness of the inner landscape and inner senses freely. This can be because there are blockages in your inner ability to perceive, due to set expectations about the workings of inner sensing and creativity.

To those to whom it comes naturally, expressing the experience often takes the form of 'I saw', 'I heard', 'I tasted', 'I smelt', 'I touched'. Therefore, if you are new to this kind of work you may expect to see, as with your outer eyes, hear, as with your outer ears, taste, as in your outer taste experience, smell as with your outer nose, and touch as with your outer sense of touch. The expectation is that everything will appear vividly and be as clear and as solid as outer reality. It is possible to feel that if you give any imaginative input into what you are seeing or experiencing as you journey in the inner worlds, that the adventures and encounters are not valid and that you are 'inventing' or 'imagining' them.

Inner worlds are very real, but this reality has its own dimension and characteristics. The way they are most usually perceived is through a sensing, a feeling and a knowing. The ability to journey into inner realities and know them is not a passive one but an active/receptive one which means that it is not something simply received but the result of an interaction. As such it is partially created by using imagination, invention and choice. There are so many permutations of the feeling or sense that you can encounter that even though you may feel you are using a rich imagination or invention, exactly *what* you imagine or invent at any given moment or life phase is bound to have important significance for you and to be influenced by your inner growth dynamic.

I am not saying that we actually imagine our Spirit Guides. They come from another dimension. Learning to be at home in, to believe in and to perceive our own inner worlds and landscape is one of the essential preparations for being able to receive and perceive this other dimension. Working to achieve a perception of our own inner worlds helps us to realise that meeting with our Spirit Guides is rarely a completely passive experience or something that happens unexpectedly of its own volition. Exercises for developing and using our inner worlds or landscape train us to be active/receptive rather than passive/receptive, which is an important mindset for achieving clear contact and close communication with our Spirit Guides.

Inner experiencing, and learning to be open to the dimension from which Spirit Guides come, is a combination of readiness, willingness, openness, trust, imagination, creativity and determination. Avoiding set expectations, as well as learning that both inner and outer perceptions are *more* than the offering of the five senses and that knowing, feeling, intuiting and sensing contribute hugely to the final vision, will help you to find your own individual way to journey into and perceive other inner and outer dimensions. You will also learn not to feel at a loss or disadvantage if at first you doubt your capacity for inner vision. Persevere, trust your ability to find a way through, and realise that perception and sensing are far, far wider than an ability to 'see'.

Keeping safe

Your inner world is actually a very safe place; it is yours and the figures in it are different parts of you. It holds that interface to other worlds that I often describe as the rainbow bridge. In the guided journeys to help you find and meet your Spirit Guide, you are taken to the place where the rainbow bridge reaches into your inner landscape so that you can experience this magical place and stand at the rainbow's beginning or end. This is perfectly possible in inner, but not outer, reality. This rainbow place can be used for healing and inspiration and as a meeting place. So far, I have suggested that you do not invite a Spirit Guide to come to the rainbow meeting place (exercise 5, Chapter 4, page 64). This is because it is advisable to get used to travelling to the level of awareness that the rainbow bridge represents and to become able to hold your consciousness and your focus at that level. (An alternative means of training yourself to focus at this level of awareness, by using your chakras, is given in exercise 7, Chapter 7, page 122.)

When you can do this, and it is not difficult to master, then you can invite your Spirit Guide to come into your landscape, to this meeting place, as explained in exercise 6, below. It is important that your Guide comes into your landscape and that you do not attempt to cross the rainbow bridge to other dimensions. Crossing into or travelling to other dimensions requires more training, preferably in the presence of an actual outer teacher experienced in such work. Therefore, you familiarise yourself with your inner world or landscape, which is another dimension of yourself and your inner experience, so that you can invite your Spirit Guide to the level where your inner and higher dimensions make such a meeting and communication possible. Your Guide, then, is always moving into your territory, you are not attempting to journey to your Guide's territory or dimension. Your Guide may not come immediately, or you may receive some sense of a presence extremely quickly, especially if you remember the advice given above about perception in the inner worlds and having an open expectation.

Power animals and travelling accompanied

Animals are significant allies in our inner worlds. They can help and guard us when we are doing work that entails possible altered states of consciousness and exploration of new territories and other realities. In the inner worlds, creatures who in the present conditions of the everyday world would be wild, fierce or unapproachable are our friends. They readily communicate, come when we call and offer healing, comfort and protection. Calling an animal to you means that you will receive help and support in keeping alert all your instinctual qualities and perceptions. In the Native American tradition they are called power or medicine animals. If we are open to them as we work in the inner worlds, a number of animals may come to us for different purposes, such as healing, guardianship, comfort, aiding communication and offering a loving companionship along the way. It is helpful to invite a special 'journey animal' to meet us on each journey, once we start developing the way to connection with our Spirit Guides. In exercise 6 the opportunity to meet such a power animal is explained. This animal will be the guardian of your threshold, making your journeys to new interfaces, and eventually new territories, extra safe and as smooth as possible.

On journeys that lead to meeting our Spirit Guides, then, we travel accompanied. We have already learned to invite our inner wise presence or being to journey with us, as explained in exercise 3, Chapter 4, page 58. A power animal, which may appear specifically to be your guardian on such journeys, can now also be included.

Whenever I am in contact with Gildas, I have a female leopard and a black panther, one on each side of me.

The rainbow bridge might also be described as a rainbow gateway, and your power animal acts as a gatekeeper, protecting you from harm. The rainbow bridge *is* both a threshold and an interface. The worlds and energies beyond it are of a different substance than either the everyday outer world or your inner landscape. If you stand within your inner landscape, with your inner wise being or presence strongly beside you, and your power animal/gatekeeper with you, then your threshold will be guarded and you will not unwittingly step into any strange worlds or dimensions beyond your understanding or your ability to handle. Any true Spirit Guide will expect you to be protected and accompanied in this way and will also expect to come into your landscape, via the rainbow bridge or gateway and will not call you beyond it until, or unless, you are well trained and prepared for such an adventure. Some people find that they have a 'gatekeeper' guide rather than, or as well as, a special power animal for this work. This guide, usually met quite naturally at the entrance to the rainbow bridge, is a guardian and not a communicating, teaching or healing guide. If such a guide appears their role will become clear, quite naturally. Your gatekeeper may also be an angelic being or your personal guardian angel.

Your own Spirit Guide also takes a part in protecting you and keeping you safe at the threshold of other worlds. There is a built-in safety mechanism in that your Guide will usually only come to you at a meeting place when you have made the journey of preparation to be there. The journey to the meeting place is about shifting your level of consciousness. Learning to make this journey with awareness creates safety and establishes the ground and focus where you and your Guide can meet. It is possible to have alternative meeting places than the rainbow bridge, and exercise 9, Chapter 9, page 155 enables you to create such a place.

The sacred law of three

In the spiritual realms there is a sacred law of three: ask for something three times and it will usually be granted. One of the ways in which guidance manifests itself is through something that will help to provide a solution to your dilemma; or you may find that an answer to your current question is brought to your attention three times in a short period.

When working with a Guide it is important to establish a recognition sign or signal that is the seal of genuineness. If we ask for such a sign when our Guide approaches, it will be shown, withdrawn, shown again, withdrawn and finally shown for a third time. Training ourselves to focus at the right level of awareness already means that there is safety from being approached by any lower entity, but also, if by any chance the focus has slipped, no false guide can abuse the law of three. None but our true Spirit Guides or benign communicators from the other worlds can maintain a threefold signal in this way.

The sign may be a fragrance, gesture, colour, symbol, or keyword; it will never be intrusive. Always remember that true Spirit Guides have a natural 'courtesy' and will not impinge their presence on us in any way that might be distasteful. Eventually, as contact and trust with our Spirit Guides develop, there can be a wonderful experience of merging with them, but this never happens until *we* are ready or *we* invite it.

Issues of discipline and the inner critic

Establishing the threefold call sign or challenge is an important tool but also an important discipline. Until we have more experience, it is not always possible to check our level of consciousness conclusively. Also, if we are in real need our Spirit Guides may step closer to our material realms where other interference or psychic 'noise' is possible. When we build in the threefold sign or signal, our Guides can know that we are safe and protected from any possible unwanted impostors or intruders.

79

Here, a word on discipline along the way to connection with Spirit Guides is needed. It is a good idea to build a rhythm or regularity into any work you are doing towards the goal of meeting your Guide, but in any scheme of such work it is essential to build in the patterns that will give you a sense of success and accomplishment rather than a sense of failing or not being 'good enough'.

Earlier in this chapter I referred to the many voices we have within us and the inner dialogues that we hold with ourselves. We all have an inner critic. This inner voice tends to give us negative, rather than constructive criticism. If we decide in our first flush of enthusiasm that we will get up half an hour earlier every day to build this work into our already busy lives, or that we will practise at least five times a week, then at the first moment that this expectation of ourselves breaks down, the negative critical voice will subtly but certainly feed back 'failure' messages to us.

If, on the other hand, we make a more relaxed and realistic plan for the work, we might say: 'I will do this as often as I can; at least once a month, but hopefully more often', then each time we do an exercise, or light a candle, or write something in our special Guide journal, the subtle messages we give ourselves will be of accomplishment. In this way we can increase the degree to which we enjoy or delight in the experience and therefore the degree to which we want to repeat it and make it a part of our lives. There will be no exacting targets to meet and no self-blame because an over-rigid system has broken down. We will build in more regularity and consistency quite naturally, with a sense of contentment and expansion, and no temptation to give up too soon because we are trying to meet unrealistic expectations of ourselves.

There *is* a necessity for discipline in this work, however, but it should not be interpreted as the need to apply an over-rigid programme for our self-growth sessions. Instead it applies to paying attention to detail, to learning to reach the right level of awareness, to appreciating the reasons for, and therefore observing, the built-in safety messages in the exercises given here so that we develop a fine focus and respect for the work.

Cultivating the inner observer

As we work to build communication with our Spirit Guides we are working towards being more finely attuned to all aspects of life and to the ways in which we can actively participate in making life more multi-dimensional, meaningful, complete and fulfilled. A harsh inner critic can be an obstacle and challenge along the way, but developing an inner, non-judgemental observer is an important asset in all spiritual growth, especially in the search for working with Spirit Guides.

This inner observer sharpens our ability to notice and interpret what is happening in both our inner and outer lives. It helps us to make connections and interpretations and to focus on the subtle messages that may be coming towards us. These will be there even before conscious connection with our Spirit Guides has been sought or achieved and will increase as we become fully engaged with the process.

The inner observer is like a mirror. When we check our appearance, a mirror itself makes no comment, judgement or decision; however, by looking in the mirror we may notice something that is out of place, needs adjusting, or is less or more enhancing than we may have thought. It is the same with the inner observer. It reflects back to us the things that are happening in our lives and makes us notice them more precisely. Then *we* can decide what changes to make whilst also being alive to subtleties that are important in expanding our perception of, and interaction with, our own growth processes.

Daily reviewing

A good way to cultivate this inner observer is to set up a regular practice of daily reviewing. Once or twice a week for a month to six weeks, before going to sleep, take your special journal and simply write down each event from your day. It is a good idea to record these moving backwards from the point where you are now, rather than starting at the beginning of the day and writing them in sequence from that point. You are less likely to miss things if you work backwards through the day. Discipline yourself to write down *only* the events, with no commentary on how you felt or how you evaluate any of the day's happenings, or your actions or reactions.

When you have a few of these lists or daily reviews, you can look through them and think about what is revealed about your life. You can also start to do a different kind of review where you write the events of the day with no comment, as before, in one column and your comments, feelings or observations about each event in a second column on the page. These records of events and feelings or comments should be, as far as is possible, without self-judgement, only observation and detached recording. Gradually you will find yourself noticing and noting details that you might previously have let pass, and that you will be training that part of yourself that is able to watch the events of your life non-judgementally to alert you to things that might have escaped your attention before. In this way you will become more mindful, more fully present in every moment and more able to differentiate between judgement and discernment. This will, in turn, help to enhance your perception of, and receptivity to, the most subtle communications from your Spirit Guide.

Before moving on to exercise 6, which is the core exercise for establishing the basic guidance journey to the place where you are most likely to be able to meet your Spirit Guide, here is Melanie's story. It is an example of someone who at first found great difficulty in perceiving her inner worlds and landscape, but who learned how to blend memory and creativity to enable them to open for her.

Melanie's story: overcoming difficulties in visualising
Although Melanie very much wanted to meet her Spirit Guide she was adamant that she could not visualise. I led her through exercise 3, Chapter 4, page 58. She found it useful in enabling her to reach a certain point of awareness and to retain her focus of attention at that point. After practising it for a while, during the time of focus she began to receive 'thought' responses to questions she had

formulated and also felt that her Spirit Guide was definitely there, although she could not describe him. Gradually she realised that every time she could focus for long enough at the required level she was no longer alone. She began to write down her thoughts when her Guide was present and received some meaningful communications that were evidential for her; she said: 'These are completely not my style and there is definitely information here that is beyond my usual knowledge. Since my imagination is not very fertile, it is also beyond anything I could imagine.'

The outcome of Melanie's efforts and practice was exciting and satisfying but still she yearned to journey in her inner landscape and have that richness as part of her potential. Because the meadow is the inner place of transition, I asked her if perhaps there was a meadow or special place she had ever spent time in or remembered. She said there was a special picnic place from her childhood. In the summer, her mother would pack sandwiches and drinks for her and her brother and sister, and they would go to a nearby field where there were beautiful trees and sometimes sheep grazing.

I asked Melanie whether she was picturing this place or remembering its sounds and smells or atmosphere most. After a few moments' thought and in rather a surprised way, she said:

The sounds and smell are important and, since it was usually a sunny day when we went to this place, the warmth of the sun on my skin and wearing only light clothing are important and I can sense that. As I let myself remember those things though, I suddenly find that I am *there* again. I know it is a memory, but I can re-enter the whole atmosphere.

I then suggested to Melanie that she could practise visualising by using this remembered experience. As she did so, on a regular basis, her imagination began to respond and she could add other features to her picnic place that were not a part of the original place or part of her memory. In this way, she began to create her inner landscape. The picnic place had a river running through it and a pathway from it that led towards some hilly areas. Gradually she built up her ability to follow the basic guidance journey (exercise 6, below) in her own way but with immense satisfaction. She continued to feel that visualisation and 'seeing' her inner worlds were still not easy for her. She felt that she had to build her own inner landscape but her inner territory gradually extended. It became more and more alive, and her enjoyment of using it continued to increase.

If you are persistent and creative in trying different approaches there *is* a way into your inner worlds. As I said before, they are *part* of you and as you find a way to make yourself known to them, they will respond by making their features more clearly accessible to you.

Exercise 6: *Meeting your power animal and Spirit Guide*

It is time now to set out the basic guidance journey in full. This journey builds on the journey taken in exercise 5, Chapter 4, page 64 and includes the opportunity to meet your power animal and to establish signs and signals to help you to identify and trust any Spirit Guide you may meet. Make the initial preparations explained in exercise 1, Chapter 4, page 54.

1. Become aware of the rhythm of your breathing and gradually bring that rhythm into your heart centre or chakra, which is in the centre of your body on the same level as your physical heart.

2. Travel on your heart energy breath into your inner landscape and find yourself in your meadow. Activate all your inner senses so that you see the objects and the colours, smell the fragrances, hear the sounds, touch the textures and savour the tastes.

3. Invite your inner wise being or presence to be with you and also have with you any special object or talisman you wish to take on this journey.

4. Look out at the surrounding landscape and see a lush, green, wooded area, perhaps in a slight valley. It is here that your power animal dwells. Within the forest there may be a rocky area with some caves or maybe some of the great trees have hollows in their trunks forming suitable places for animals to live. Accompanied by your inner wise presence or being, journey to the forest area and call your animal to come to you. Remember that this creature is your friend and ally, even though it may be one of the big cats, a wolf or a deadly snake. Greet your animal and ask it to accompany you on your journey to meet the presence of your Spirit Guide.

5. Emerge from your forest to a place where you can see the winding pathway that leads into the hills and continues up into the mountains. Take this pathway, knowing that you are going to the plateau that is near the top, but not at the top, of one of the higher hills or mountains.

6. At the plateau, refresh yourself from the source of clear running water, visit the travellers' rest that may be here and then notice again the place where the rainbow bridge meets the earth or rock of your plateau. Enter the rainbow light, feel its healing vitalisation, settle yourself comfortably within it, whilst your inner wise presence and your animal guardian wait nearby. It may be that at this entrance to the rainbow bridge you sense the presence of a guardian or gatekeeper guide or an angelic guardian, who will greet you and welcome you into the centre of the rainbow light and then take up the guardianship stance once more.

7. Breathe again into your heart chakra, so that your heart energy flows strongly, and wait with an open expectation.

8. In your heart, speak an invitation or invocation for your Guide to appear. Affirm your readiness for this contact and connection.

9. Be aware that a being may come to join you in this rainbow light. This being may appear in a particular dress from a particular geographic area or historical time or it may come in a body of light and colour, as a fragrance or merely as a sense of another energy being present with you – a knowledge that you are not alone.

10. In whatever form your Guide elects to appear you should feel a sense of openness and peace. You may feel excited or perhaps a little anxious, but the very ambience of your Guide's presence should be reassuring and comforting.

11. Ask now for a sign or signal to be shown and clearly repeated to you three times. When the signal has been given, greet your Guide and ask any questions you might have in your mind. At this point you might like to ask for a name for your Guide. Remember that you may get a response in words, symbols or inner knowing. You may only feel a sense of continuing peace. In this case trust that in the next few days there will be synchronicities or coincidences in your life that will evoke the answers, responses or guidance you seek.

12. Stay here for no more than 15 minutes. When you are ready to return, drink again from the water source on your plateau and then, accompanied by your inner wise presence and your power animal, make your way back to the

meadow, where you take leave of your companions and return to your physical awareness of your breath in your heart centre.

13. Become conscious of your body, your connection with the ground and your outer surroundings.

14. Visualise a cloak of light with a hood, right around you.

15. Take time to record your journey in your special book before returning to your everyday routines.

You now have in place all the basic exercises for developing contact with your Spirit Guide. Chapter 6 looks at the need to recognise the many ways in which guidance may be made manifest for us.

6

Guidance is Everywhere

This chapter looks at the many ways in which guidance might be received, including the rich world of dreams. Even as we begin the search for closer contact with our personal Spirit Guides we may already be in touch with considerable amounts of guidance. There are as many indirect ways of being guided as there are of the more direct forms of communication. We are already looked after and overseen long before we meet our Guides as friends. Our lives have a shape that is not dependent on formal or clear connection with our Spirit Guides, our higher selves or our guardian angels; we don't live in a vacuum. Learning to see the ways in which we are already guided, or the subtle ways in which our Guides may already be communicating with us, can help strengthen the bridge that makes the guidance connection more conscious as well as giving us more tools to access the wider perspectives we seek.

Guidance from life itself

In exercise 4, Chapter 4, page 60, as you asked the question: 'Where am I now?', you took an overview of your life. Perhaps at the time, you were able to see patterns of guidance and synchronicity in your life, leading you to lessons you are here to learn. If you look back at this overview now, and perhaps extend your thoughts and reflections on it, you will see more of how the pattern of life itself constitutes guidance.

If you accept that, as most Spirit Guides say, there are no mistakes but only learning experiences, you can look more clearly at what life has taught you and at how you can use clearer and more conscious contact with your Spirit Guide to become a co-creator in its course.

In many senses our Guides are endeavouring to contact us before we contact them. Life often seems to guide us by knocks on the head and kicks from behind. Having conscious access to our Guides and learning to see more clearly the signs and signals life gives us *before* the knocks on the head or kicks from behind are necessary can help to ensure that our lives run more smoothly. In so far as Spirit Guides agonise over us, their charges, they particularly do so when we make vital life changes or learn to look after ourselves only through having life crises of one kind or another.

Throughout the book so far we have looked at building the bridge to direct channelling from a specific Guide or source. Let us now look at the other ways in which guidance or Guides may be seeking to reach us or speak to us.

Direct channelling

I use this term to describe the sort of channelling that happens in direct response to a request for contact with a Spirit Guide. The channeller has consciously asked for the connection to happen, and receives the guidance immediately as a flowing response. The chan-neller may know and speak the words that the guide is transmitting. This is how my channelling of Gildas usually works. I shift my level of awareness, become aware that Gildas is responding or ready to communicate and then receive into my head, like dictation, the words that Gildas is using. When I first received these direct and fluent communications at the age of 19, a certain shyness prevented me from saying aloud what I was receiving, and as it reminded me so much of a process of dictation, I trained myself to write quickly and recorded it in longhand on paper. I was not fully conscious of the content of what I had written until I read it, or someone else read it out afterwards. This was not, however, what is known in esoteric fields as 'automatic writing'. This latter is an energetic phenomenon, more 'in vogue' in the séances of Victorian times. In automatic writing, the pen is held by the medium or channel, but the hand that holds the pen is moved over the paper by some other energy or volition, the writer simply allowing the hand and the pen to be moved. The result is usually difficult to read and the words may have no spaces between them. The handwriting is usually quite unlike the recipient's own.

When receiving channelling from Gildas in this way, my hand-writing is very much my own, I become aware of the words and the phrases and write down what I am receiving, and the only energy moving the pen or pressing the keys on the computer is mine. As I have grown more confident and outgoing, I now usually speak the words that Gildas is communicating to me into a tape recorder, so that there is a record of what has been said. In this modern world of technology, when people at a distance want a channelling session it can be performed by post or e-mail; I then receive the words in the same way, but type them into the computer.

Whilst the channelling is happening, I am completely aware of each word and phrase and often know that Gildas is searching for a certain precise word in order to imprint that and no other into my awareness. The reason why I am not aware of the total content of what has been communicated when a session has finished is because I *am* in an altered state of consciousness. Even though the change is minimal, the process of receiving each word and phrase is so intense that I lose touch with the coherence of the whole.

After a session of channelling, I liken my feeling to the feeling that sometimes comes after a dream. The dream itself may be vivid and I awake determined to write it down, but if I then go to the bath-room or to make a cup of tea first, it has slipped away beyond recall. After a session, when people are talking about what Gildas has communicated, I can sometimes vaguely remember some of the content, but I could not give any sort of reliable résumé. For this reason, unless a session is being written or typed, it is tape-recorded for later transcription.

Direct channelling, which is that received in the moment of a knowing contact with a Spirit Guide, can be spoken, written, received as symbols or as inner knowing. Rather than writing or speaking words that have been coherently received, the channeller, because he or she is in an altered state of awareness, might say: 'I am being told that …' and then describe in his or her own words a knowledge or viewpoint that is being given or shown. Equally the channeller may say: 'I am being given …' and then go on to describe a symbolic gift, or image or keyword. Some channels draw and then describe the experience of the drawing, sharing what has been drawn with the person seeking guidance.

A degree of altered consciousness almost always accompanies direct channelling, enabling receptivity to an input that is other than our own thought processes. For the kind of channelling that people are interested in developing now, this altered state of consciousness is usually a light and not a deep trance state. It is a state of enhanced awareness rather than a sleepy state. Ideally it is a state where, although we are *aware* of what is happening in the world around us, it does not impinge or disturb our personal or internal process. When I channel Gildas, for example, I am aware if the tape in the tape recorder comes to an end and can take responsibility for turning it over or changing it. I am aware if the phone rings, or someone comes to the door and can choose what I do about these occurrences without breaking the connection with Gildas's flow of words. If I *do* decide to break off in order to deal with the phone or a caller, I am not energetically shaken or disturbed by the need for a quick change in levels. When I resume, Gildas usually takes up exactly where he left off, even if it is mid-sentence. These sometimes enforced or necessary transitions are easier than the transition from sleeping to waking, for example.

In an over-altered state of consciousness or a deeper trance, interruptions and sudden returns can be deeply disturbing, and if a medium works from such states it is usually necessary to have someone near them to help both the transition into the deep state and the return phase from it. One of the definitions of the difference between cooperative and interactive channelling and mediumship is connected to the level of change in consciousness. The exercises in this book for achieving the right level of awareness are designed to help in arriving at a lightly altered state of consciousness and expansion. If you think you want to learn more about trance mediumship it is advisable to find a specialist teacher or group (see also Glossary: **Altered state (of consciousness)**).

Hunches and intuition

I hope that all readers of this book at sometime in their lives have experienced that wonderfully creative and exciting insight or realisation that comes from a hunch or intuition. These terms usually refer to a sudden perception, knowing, or creative idea that leads to a resolution of something pressing, or a whole new sense of direction. It is the happening that is sometimes termed the 'eureka' experience. It is a peak moment that can be attributed to all kinds of previous perceptions and knowledge suddenly coming together in one amazing moment of recognition. It is not necessarily the result of a conscious and clearly thought-out request for guidance. Nor is it possible to say definitively whether it comes from inner guidance or revelation, from soul or higher self-guidance or from a communication with a Spirit Guide. It is not possible to plan it or make it happen. Nevertheless, I do believe that Spirit Guides often use this phenomenon as a means of 'touching' us, when we have made a request or expressed a longing. I believe our Spirit Guides have the power to bestow this kind of experience upon us. One of the benefits of writing your day reviews and activating your inner observer, as I discuss later in this chapter, is that you will notice whether such experiences are increased in your life as you pursue your guidance quest. In this way you can sense whether your guide is using this as a way of communicating with you.

Synchronicity

In the *Chambers Dictionary* synchronise is defined as: 'to coincide or agree in time'; 'to *cause* to coincide or agree in time' (the italics here are mine). I firmly believe that Spirit Guides have an input into causing things to coincide or agree in time, either *before* we seek to become consciously aware of guidance in our lives or in order to give us the answers we seek when we *have* wittingly taken on that search. They will help us to be in the right place at the right time. As part of their search to make contact with us they may use synchronicity to make us aware of the phenomenon of guidance.

Synchronicity may mean meeting the right person at the right time, finding the right book at the right time, hearing the right thing at the right time or reading the right notice at the right time. It might even be that coming across this book was a synchronicity of this kind in your life – a signal perhaps from your Guides that they are journeying towards contact with you and that they want you to take your part of the journey towards contact with them and to finding the meeting place.

People often meet each other and make a meaningful lifetime contact by attending the same workshop or meeting. In one workshop I held in France, at which 12 people were present, three of them felt that they had met for a special purpose, a project they agreed to undertake together. They felt that they had been looking for each other for quite a period of time. They then realised that two years previously they had all attended a large conference elsewhere, and that before that all three of them had been present at a similar large event. Eventually they came to wonder if their Guides had been extremely busy trying to arrange synchronicity for them, but finally in some kind of guidance desperation had had to bring them to a small workshop where they could not avoid making the contact and recognition that was so meaningful and productive for them all. As a result of this meeting they decided to work together and eventually set up a successful project for organising spiritual events and dialogues between speakers from different spiritual persuasions.

Synchronicity often uses the 'law of three' (see also Chapter 5, page 79); this is where things happen or impinge on our awareness three times in relatively quick succession. I have learned that notic- ing this and acting on it can result in guidance of a particularly clear and relevant kind.

Dreams

The Talmud says that 'Dreams are messages from our Souls'. Psychologists such as Sigmund Freud and C. G. Jung placed great importance on the need to understand our dreams as a means to deeper understanding of ourselves. Ancient and some so-called more primitive cultures also greatly value dreams and the dreamers of dreams. The ancient Egyptians and Greeks used dream interpreta- tion as an aid to healing maladies of both body and soul.

We spend about a third of our lives in sleep and quite a sizeable proportion of sleep time is dreaming time. We all dream. Scientific sleep analysis has determined that we do so regularly in certain phases of sleep. Those who maintain: 'I never dream', actually mean that they never remember their dreams. Many who regularly remember dreams despair of ever being able to understand their confused nature and sometimes obscure symbolism.

Whether we remember our dreams or not, they play a part in keeping us healthy. In experiments where volunteers were consis- tently deprived of dreaming sleep but allowed good periods of non-dreaming sleep, poor concentration, irritability and periods of hallucination resulted. Those who were allowed dreaming sleep, but allowed less sleep time in total than would normally be thought necessary, managed well and maintained good focus and concentra- tion levels.

Scientists believe that whilst we dream our brains are sifting through our reactions to life and its events, sorting through and storing them. We may find it difficult to admit to some of our reac- tions and responses to life during full conscious awareness; we therefore censor them and push them down deep into our psyche.

Part of a dream's content is related to the memory of this sorting and sifting process, and the seemingly obscure symbolism within dreams occurs because of our censoring process. To be brought into full awareness, these deep inner observations require self-work and openness, but the process can be richly rewarding in expanding self-knowledge and spiritual growth.

As dreams hold such important communications for us, both from within our psyches and from dimensions beyond, it is well worth the effort required to improve our dream recall and to learn to understand and appreciate the rich symbols dreams give us more fully.

When we become more at home in the territory of dreams, our Spirit Guides as well as our souls will sometimes use dreams as a means of showing us a way forward or of sending us a message that otherwise our more conscious mental processes might block. We can even learn to 'incubate' a dream as a means of obtaining guidance or understanding, as I discuss later in this chapter.

I would certainly recommend that for those intent on building the bridge to Spirit Guides, attention to dreams should be part of the journey. Studying our dreams helps us to be more flexible in our thinking and to understand the power and wonder of symbols. This is not the place to write a full guide to dream recall and interpretation. However, some simple measures often suffice to make us much more conversant with the rich language of dreams. If you want to make a fuller study, see books recommended in Further Reading.

If you want to learn to remember your dreams, have a notebook and pen beside your bed and, immediately you wake, write down your first thoughts. Make a note of the feeling quality you sense as you wake. If there is some vaguely remembered 'snippet' of a dream, do not dismiss it, but write it down. Doing this will signal to your psyche that you want to listen to, and partake in, the dialogue of your dreams.

At first, don't try to understand or interpret your dreams, unless you are used to doing so. Simply notice whatever you can, note it down and, from time to time, re-read and reflect on what you have written and what you have learned from and about your dream life. We dream roughly every one and a half hours during sleep, so if you feel that you are not getting enough dream material into your memory and wish to do so, you could try setting an alarm to wake you about one and a half hours after you go to sleep. Waking as you are dreaming, or immediately after a dreaming phase, will usually give you some material to write down and to be able to work with.

The more you write things down and simply reflect on what you have written, the more will you begin to get a sense of the messages held within your dreams. Sometimes sharing such a process with a friend or partner will help to open up the dream language even before you endeavour to learn more about symbols.

Symbols, even apart from dreams, can play an important part in guidance. Most Spirit Guides will include symbols in their guidance, and some may only communicate through the giving of symbols, as I discuss later in this chapter. However, when interpreting symbols, especially from dreams, be wary of books that give you such emphatic information as 'snakes are sexual symbols' or, 'dreaming of ladders means you will be going up or down in the world'.

Before you look up the meaning of a symbol you need to make your own associations to it. Has this symbol occurred in your life before? Does it remind you of anything? Even without knowing its meaning, does it touch you deeply? This process is known as 'association'. When you have exhausted your associations to the symbol, have a look at it again in the context of the dream and see whether the meaning of the dream may already have opened up a little. At this stage, you can go to a symbol book, but use one that gives both meanings and derivations for the symbol, not one that is only about dream symbolism (see Further Reading). Such books give the history of symbols and what they can mean in different cultures. See whether anything that is said here resonates with you, and whether such a resonance makes your dream more meaningful. You could also ask other people how they would understand the symbol and so build up your understanding of it and why your dreaming self might have used it now. This process is known as 'amplification'.

Dreams are clever, and everything in them has meaning. One way of looking at dreams is to see every part of the dream as a part of yourself. In this way you never assume that if you dream about a friend, partner or relative, the dream is telling you something about that individual. The dream's messages are for you, and so it is important to reflect upon what that person means for you. The question to ask is: 'What does this person teach me about myself?'

Numbers in dreams may refer to certain years in your life, or take you back to different ages. They may refer to a number of days, weeks or months previously, as well as to years. Words in dreams may also be puns or contain 'word play' (see the dream example on page 99).

Because most things in dreams are symbolic, dreams that contain death or birth do not necessarily mean that an actual death or birth is about to occur. A dream about death may be telling you, quite positively, that something in your life needs to be left behind or allowed to 'die' symbolically. Birth types of dream may tell you that you can give birth to a whole new phase in your life or to something creative and new.

Some people *do* have precognitive dreams in which they see something happening and then later it takes place, just as the dreamer dreamed. This is a comparatively rare phenomenon, but if you have had such a dream it is all too easy to assume that most of your dreams will in some way be precognitive. This may not be an entirely comfortable feeling to live with. I would therefore advise you to consult a counsellor who is experienced in dream work to help to put these kinds of dreams into perspective and to make you feel more comfortable with your dreaming self and the riches dreams can reveal.

Incubating a dream

Once you become interested in your dreams, you will realise how fertile they can be in giving you self-knowledge and a higher perspective. It is then worth endeavouring to 'incubate' a dream for guidance when you have a perplexing issue to explore. The law of three applies again, as explained in chapter 5, page 79. I usually light a candle three nights running, just before I go to bed. As I light the candle, I focus on the issue I want to explore more deeply and ask my dreaming self, in conjunction with Gildas or my soul, to give me a dream about it. Then I sit quietly with the candle for another two or three minutes and then blow it out, to activate my dreaming self. Sometimes the dream comes immediately on the first night, sometimes it does not come even on the third night, but, nevertheless, I light the candle only three times for this purpose. The dream rarely fails to come, even if it is two or three weeks later, but 'nagging' at the dreaming self does not work. It will respond in its own time.

Joy's story: interpreting a dream:
A counselling client of mine, Joy, dreamed that she was getting married. She had arrived at the church, which was situated at the end of a road marked 'No Through Road' in the village of Nokey, in an old car, driven by herself. She was wearing a long yellow dress, rather than the traditional white. She knew she was here to get married, but realised that she did not know who she was about to marry. A woman at the church gate told her that there was no need to worry about the bridegroom not turning up, because he and his best man were already in the church. Feeling that she had many questions about this wedding and unsure as to whether she wanted it to go ahead, she peeped into the church through the open doors: there were no guests or witnesses; the woman at the gate was only an onlooker. The bridegroom and his best man were indeed at the front of the church. They had taken off their jackets and my client could see that they were wearing very old-fashioned trousers, high at the back and held only by old-fashioned braces, not by a belt. Joy described them as 'country yokel' trousers and found them off-putting. The groom and best man in the dream were also much older than Joy. She decided to leave without going ahead with the wedding or even communicating with the bridegroom. When she went to

her car, however, she discovered that it had changed. It was brand new and a different make but she knew it was hers because her things were in it and the car keys in her handbag fitted it. The name of the model of the new car was 'Swift'. Joy's feeling on awakening from the dream was one of exhilaration as she realised that her new car was powerful and exciting to drive.

At that time in her life, Joy, a young solicitor, had been offered a partnership in the firm of solicitors with whom she had been employed for a number of years. She was undecided, realising that the offer of a partnership was a great privilege, but she feared 'tying herself in' to a somewhat old-fashioned and weighty structure. However, she felt that if she turned the offer down, she might be letting go of an opportunity that would give her security for life. This meant a lot to her, as she was an only child whose penniless parents had died before she was 20. The security the partnership would offer her would enable her to buy a home of her own and put down roots. On the other hand, she was still young and had an unfulfilled spirit of adventure. Joy was good at the work she did and realised that she could also use her skills as a gateway to many experiences and to widening her life.

As we looked at her dream, it seemed to both of us to be a clear piece of guidance about how she felt deep within herself, about the present offer and the dilemma she felt it had raised for her. The marriage represented the potential business partnership, and the dream contained some straightforward word play messages: the church was in a village called 'Nokey' or 'no key' and at the end of a 'No Through Road'.

Cars in dreams can be seen as 'portable psychic space'. The car Joy was driving herself to the wedding in, unsupported and alone, was an old one. We noted again the word play in: 'driving herself'. Her association to the car was that it was similar to a car her parents had once had. They had all valued it, because, for parents who had always struggled on a low income, having a car at all was a great thrill and achievement, but it was certainly an old model and from an earlier phase of her life; the car model itself had long been discontinued. She felt that the symbol of the car showed her that she partly wanted to take the offered partnership because she knew it would have pleased her parents so much and would have been much what they wanted for her. She realised that even though her parents were now dead, she would be taking the partnership partly to please them. If they had still been alive, this career step for Joy would also have meant that she could ease her parents' financial burden and so feel that she was repaying them for the sacrifices they had made for her, especially when it came to her further education. It did not take much prompting on my part for Joy to see that because circumstances had changed these reasons for taking the partnership were now redundant, like the model of the car.

Joy's associations to the yellow dress were firstly that, although she *liked* yellow as a colour and used it in her living space, she knew that she certainly did not look her best in it and therefore never wore it. She remembered that when she was 14 years old she had been invited to her first 'grown up' party that was going on until quite late in the evening and where she knew all her friends were going to 'dress up'. She had longed for a suitable 'evening dress', but knew her parents could not really afford to get her one. Eventually her mother had mentioned the matter to an aunt, who happened to have a long yellow satin dress that fitted Joy perfectly. At first, she was overjoyed, but when she wore it, she realised, even then, that yellow was not the most flattering colour for her and that although the dress was lovely, it was by no means as perfect as she had first thought.

In the dream Joy is told by the woman at the church gate that the bridegroom was already there in the church, but Joy felt unsure about the wedding, especially when she saw the bridegroom and best man were much older than herself and were wearing old-fashioned clothes. Also, there were no guests or witnesses present.

Here again the dream is reiterating how everything is somehow related to a past time and that Joy herself has no family support. She realised that the firm of solicitors was old-fashioned and that no one she knew would celebrate with her if she accepted the offer. The bridegroom and best man had their jackets off and she found their old-fashioned clothes off-putting. Usually clothes in dreams symbolise how we 'dress' for the world, and when we take layers off we show what is beneath the surface. With their jackets off, the bridegroom and best man were revealing an old-fashioned underlying structure.

After Joy decided not to go ahead with the wedding she went back to her car, her 'portable psychic space', and saw that it was a new car, with the model name of 'Swift'.

The dream was clear guidance indeed about what Joy's true self was really thinking about the offer of partnership. If she took it she would be trapped in an old structure as well as firmly wedded to her work. The bridegroom and best man, representing the senior partners in the business, were more than ready to welcome her into this partnership. She was a bright prospect for them and would bring new energy to the company, but in the dream even Joy's wedding dress did not suit her and was associated with a difficult rite of passage from childhood to the more adult world. When she resolutely walked away from the church, there was a transformation. By not going ahead with the 'wedding' she had got herself a new portable psychic space that would take her swiftly through life and on to a new adventure. Needless to say, Joy turned the partnership down. Shortly afterwards she was offered a new position with a go-ahead firm of solicitors. It did not have the status of a partnership but did give her the opportunity for travel and for widening her learning and experience.

Dreams are rich and, what I would call, 'economical'. Joy's dream provided a wealth of symbols that, in the circumstances, iterated and reiterated that if she took the partnership she would be stuck in a very old-fashioned framework and would compromise her freedom and her speed of movement through life. However, it also had other layers of meaning for her at that particular phase of her life.

In self-development, one of the important things to look at is the inner balance between the energy of the masculine and feminine principles. Masculine principle might be defined as 'focused attention' and feminine principle as 'diffuse awareness'. Joy was in a very masculine principle area of work and the firm that valued her so much was run on particularly old-fashioned masculine principle lines. Joy herself felt 'driven', as well as driving herself (as to the wedding in the dream). She felt driven to do well in her career but the dream helped her to realise that it was her parents' values, particularly those of her father, and her concern for her parents that was a major driving force for her.

In looking at the other messages the dream might be giving, as well as the clear, directional guidance, Joy saw that she had not truly finished mourning her parents. They had died before she had reached a point in her career where she could have helped them financially to a better quality of life and she had not yet left her regrets and anguish about this behind. She was carrying an old-fashioned structure within, driving in an old, heavy, unwieldy car, on the brink of making a decision for reasons that were now redundant, not claiming or honouring her own potential for her own sake. When she talked further about the new car, named 'Swift', she said it was a very 'snazzy' convertible. Although it had masculine principle speed and thrust, it nevertheless made her feel feminine, with its graceful lines and the opportunity it would give to let her hair blow free in the breeze.

The dream was guiding her not only about the impending important decision but also about letting the past go, so that she could move on in her life, including developing a new relationship with herself and giving herself permission to have more fun and spontaneity. It is a perfect example of the multi-faceted guidance of dreams.

In the next chapter I give a brief explanation of chakra energies and our subtle bodies, as a guide to understanding different levels of awareness and changes of consciousness. With this knowledge, exercises can be given that will suit those who wish to have a less visual means of journeying to the right level of focus for contact with Spirit Guides.

7

Chakras, Subtle Bodies and Subtle Planes

This chapter is a brief introduction to chakras, subtle bodies and subtle planes. In order to receive coherent guidance from a Spirit Guide it is necessary to strengthen your subtle energy field. Often referred to as the auric field or aura, when its make-up is described in more detail the subtle field that surrounds our physical bodies can be seen to consist of chakras and subtle bodies. The diagram on page 104 shows the subtle body layers that surround the physical body, whilst the diagram on page 106 shows the positions and names of the main chakras. More detailed information about chakras and the auric field can be found in my books *Working with your Chakras* and *Energy Healing for Beginners* (see Further Reading).

When working with Spirit Guides, learning about chakras and the subtle layers of the energy field gives you information and tools with which to strengthen your aura and therefore enhance the range and strength of your subtle perceptions. Chakra knowledge can also help you to work on personal issues that may colour or block the clarity of your channelling.

The auric or energy field

We do not begin and end as individuals at the boundary around our bodies marked by our skin. Around each one of us, beyond our physical skin or substance, is a subtle energy field or aura. It consists of six levels or layers, each of which vibrates with, or resonates to, a state of being and a plane of awareness (see diagram, below). Those who are able to see auras will experience them as full of colour. Generally this auric or energy field occupies a space of 10–15 centimetres (4–6 inches) around and beyond the physical body as well as interpenetrating with our physical bodies.

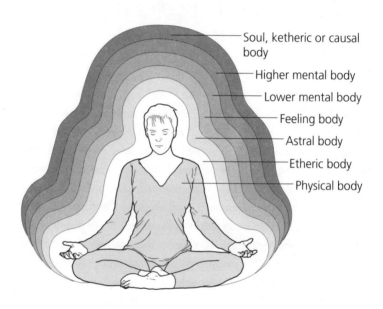

Soul, ketheric or causal body
Higher mental body
Lower mental body
Feeling body
Astral body
Etheric body
Physical body

The physical body and the six layers of the auric field

It is quite easy to sense your own energy field. Rub the palms of your hands together for a few moments and then hold them about 1 metre (3 feet) apart. Gradually bring the palms of your hands closer and closer together until you feel a slight tingling or resistance. This sensation indicates one edge of your energy field meeting the other, or the energetic poles (+ and –) interacting.

You can also experiment with sensing another willing person's energy field as they sense yours. Rub your hands together and face your partner. Hold your hands about 1 metre (3 feet) away from your partner's hands, so that your right hand is facing their left hand and your left hand is facing their right hand. Gradually bring your hands in towards each other until you encounter that slight tingling or electrical resistance that indicates that you are encountering each other's energy fields.

Much of the colour and energy of the auric field is supplied by subtle energy centres known as chakras. The word chakra comes from the Sanskrit, 'chakrum' meaning 'wheel'. Correctly speaking, chakrum is the singular form and chakra the plural, but in the West it is more usual to speak of one chakra and many chakras. People who are able to 'see' will experience chakras as subtle wheels or turning, pulsating flowers of light and colour. They are the points in our subtle energy field where universal energy enters and interpenetrates with our personal energy systems. Most chakras carry links to specific parts of our physical glandular systems and affect, and are affected by, our physical bodies and constitution.

The diagram overleaf shows the positions, names and subtle forms of the major chakras, showing how they interpenetrate with our physical bodies. The seven major chakras – crown, brow, throat, heart, solar plexus, sacral and root – are linked to the seven colours of the rainbow spectrum: violet for the crown, indigo for the brow, blue for the throat, green for the heart, yellow for the solar plexus, orange for the sacral and red for the root.

Each chakra is responsible for producing its spectrum colour to feed into the physical body and the auric field in order to keep the whole being healthy on every level. The alter major chakra, also shown in the diagram on page 106, although important in the chakra system, is technically a minor chakra, and its colours – yellow ochre, olive green and reddish brown – deviate from the normal rainbow chakra colours.

The healthy being is a radiant, rainbow being. The rainbow bridge that aids our more subtle levels of awareness helps to connect us to our higher vitality and perceptions and thus to be subtly vital enough to meet, and register, the even more vibrant energy of our Spirit Guides.

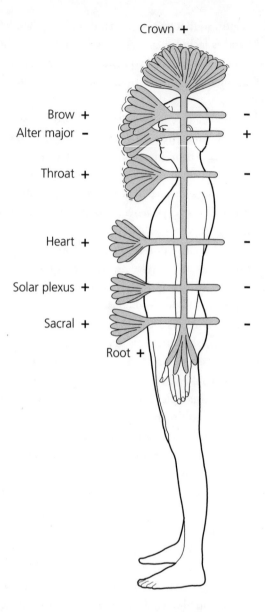

Crown +

Brow +
Alter major –

Throat +

Heart +

Solar plexus +

Sacral +

Root +

–

+

–

–

–

–

The seven best-known chakras and the alter major. Energy flows both
from positive (+) to negative (–) polarities and up and down the central
column. Note the reversed polarity of the alter major chakra.

Although each chakra needs its home spectrum colour and is responsible for the production of that colour for the whole auric field, the root chakra is not only red, the solar plexus not only yellow and so on. Each and every colour may be present in each and every chakra, but if its home colour is not also strong and flowing, then there is imbalance in the total being. Such imbalance may be temporary, due to passing emotions, stress or tiredness. Our chakras, and therefore our auras, change many times during a day and also when we sleep.

Healthy chakras and auric colours look like stained glass when sunlight passes through it: intense, bright and translucent. When there is imbalance in us, our colours may be opaque, or faint. Our colours are also related to gifts and abilities and it is natural to have more of some than of others, but when one spectrum colour is straining to maintain itself, or is almost totally absent or decidedly over-prominent, it can be a sign that all is not well.

Chakras are linked not only to colour but also to keywords, developmental stages, elements and senses, and to each of the seven 'bodies' in our auric field, to glands and fragrances and to crystals or gemstones. Informing ourselves about these connections will enable our Spirit Guides to give us chakra exercises that can help in clearing blockages in our lives and energy fields and to clearing the way to guidance contact.

In esoteric teachings there is sometimes a lack of agreement as to whether chakras are situated at the front or the back of the body and its auric field. Some systems place some chakras at the front and some at the back, whereas others place all at the front or all at the back. The illustration on page 106 depicts the way in which chakras exist both in the energy field and in interpenetration with the physical body.

Each chakra has something of the appearance of a flower, having petals and a stem. The stems of the crown and root chakras are open but are contained in a central column of energy that interpenetrates totally with our physical bodies (see exercise 1, Chapter 4, page 55). The other chakras have petals opening into the auric field at the front and stems projecting into the auric field at the back.

The stems normally stay closed, but the petals are flexible, opening and closing, vibrating and turning according to the different life situations encountered.

Positions and connections

The following section describes the body positions of the chakras and the ways in which they connect to various aspects of our lives.

Root chakra

This is located in the perineum, which is the area midway between the anus and the genitals. The petals face downwards, between the legs, and the stem faces upwards into the central column. It is naturally and healthily slightly open. The keywords are: rootedness, incarnation, acceptance, preservation and concept. It is linked to the developmental stage that takes place from birth to three or five years of age. Its main spectrum colour is red and it has secondary colours of brown and mauve. Its element is earth; its sense is smell. The root chakra is associated with the physical body and the gonad glands (testes in men and ovaries in women). The fragrances of cedarwood and patchouli will quieten and calm the root chakra, whilst musk, lavender and hyacinth will stimulate it. Its crystals are: smoky quartz, garnet, alexandrite, ruby, agate, bloodstone, onyx, tiger's eye and rose quartz (see also Further Reading for books on crystals).

Sacral chakra

This is located approximately two fingers below the navel. The stem corresponds to the sacrum area in the spine. The keywords are: security, sense of others, sexuality, creativity, power, empowerment, relationship, co-creativity and sincerity. The sacral chakra is connected with the developmental stages that take place between the ages of three or five to eight years. Its main colour is orange and the secondary colours are amber and gold. Its element is water; its sense taste. It is linked to the etheric body, as I discuss later in this chapter. The glandular connection is to the lymphatic system.

Quietening fragrances for the sacral chakra are musk and amber; rosemary and rose geranium will stimulate it. Its crystals are amber, citrine, topaz, aventurine, moonstone and jasper.

Solar plexus chakra

This is situated just below the sternum, extending down to the navel, and the stem is in the corresponding position at the back. The keywords are: logic, reason, opinion, assimilation, psychic intuition, and identity. The developmental age associated with the solar plexus chakra is from eight to 12 years. Its main colour is yellow and the secondary colours are gold and rose. The element is fire, the sense is sight and the subtle body is the astral body. The glandular connection is to the adrenals. The quietening fragrances are vetivert and rose, whilst bergamot and ylang-ylang will stimulate the solar plexus. The crystals for this chakra are: yellow citrine, apatite, calcite, kunzite, rose quartz, iron pyrites (fool's gold), yellow topaz and malachite.

Heart chakra

This is found on the same level as the physical heart but in the centre of the body, with the stem at the back. The keywords and phrases for the heart chakra are: compassion, feeling, tenderness, love of, and search for, the Divine, love of others and detachment. The associated developmental age is from 12 to 15 years. Its main colour is spring green and the subsidiary colours are rose and rose amethyst. The element is air, the sense touch, and the subtle body connection is to the feeling body. The glandular link is to the thymus. The functioning of some glands in the physical body remain something of a mystery even to modern medical science and the thymus is one of these. It is part of the lymphatic system, situated directly below the thyroid and parathyroid gland. It secretes a hormone known as thymic humoral factor. Between the ages of 12 and 15 in the maturing human the thymus gland begins to reduce in size. It is thought to have a connection with physical growth and with progression from childhood to maturity. The fragrances of rose and sandalwood quieten the heart chakra whilst pine and honey-suckle are stimulating for it. The crystals are: emerald, green calcite, amber, azurite, chrysoberyl, rose and watermelon tourmalines and jade.

Throat chakra

This is located at the neck, with the petals in front and the stem at the back. The keywords are: expression, responsibility, communication and universal truth. The developmental age is between 15 and 21 years. The main colour for the throat chakra is blue with the subsidiary colours of silver and turquoise. The element is ether, or akasha (see Glossary). The sense for the throat chakra is hearing and the subtle body is the mental body. The glandular connection is to the thyroid and parathyroid. Lavender and hyacinth are quietening fragrances for this chakra, and patchouli and white musk are its stimulants. The crystals are: lapis lazuli, aquamarine, sodalite, turquoise and sapphire.

Brow chakra

This is located above and between the eyes, with a stem at the corresponding level at the back of the head. The keywords are: spirit, completeness, inspiration, insight and command. The main colour is indigo and the subsidiary colours are turquoise and mauve. The element for the brow chakra is radium and the subtle body connection is to the higher mental. The glandular link is to the pineal gland. White musk and hyacinth are quietening fragrances for the brow, and violet and rose geranium will stimulate it. The crystals are: amethyst, purple apatite, azurite, calcite, pearl, and the purple, blue and white varieties of fluorite. There is no associated developmental stage or sense for this, or any chakra above the throat chakra.

Crown chakra

This chakra is often referred to as the 'thousand-petalled lotus'. It is situated at the top of the head, with the petals facing upwards and a stem going down into the central column. The keywords are: soul, surrender, release and incoming will. The main colour is violet, with white and gold as the subsidiary colours. The element, given by teaching Guides, is magnetum, but this has not yet been discovered for inclusion in tables of elements. The glandular connection from the crown chakra is to the pituitary, and its subtle body link is to the soul, ketheric, or causal body. The quietening fragrances are rosemary and bergamot with violet and amber as stimulants. The crystals are: diamond, white tourmaline, white jade, snowy quartz and celestite.

Alter major chakra
The alter major chakra is located with its petals in the area of the nose. Its positive energy centre is in its stem, which is situated where the back of the head begins to curve round into the neck. This location corresponds to the 'old' or 'lizard' brain, before the division into the right and left hemispheres. The keywords are: instinct, resonance, rhythm, duality, devic nature and healing. The principal colour is yellow ochre with subsidiary colours of brown ochre and olive green. The element for the alter major chakra is wet earth, and the sense, shared with the root chakra, is smell. The subtle body link is to the instinctual or lower causal body, and the glandular link, shared with the solar plexus, is to the adrenals. Musk and cedarwood fragrances quieten this chakra whilst violet and rose geranium are its stimulants. The crystals are: carnelian, tiger's eye, snowflake obsidian, fossils and peacock stone.

Chakras and our Spirit Guides

We have established the rainbow bridge as a meeting place. The colours of the seven major chakras are also a rainbow spectrum. The rainbow is a symbol of wholeness or synthesis. In esoteric understanding we learn that chakras, colours and subtle planes are also related. In seeking connection with our Spirit Guides we are also seeking to expand our understanding of ourselves and to develop the ability to focus energies that are normally unseen and unharnessed.

When we work with our chakras, even in such a simple way as feeding each major chakra with its home colour, we enhance and strengthen our auric field. This enables us to perceive and sustain connections with those higher beings unseen by physical eyes, who are our Spirit Guides. When we take the whole of our rainbow selves to the rainbow bridge, then we enable connections to be made and synchronicities to happen. Working to keep our chakras in optimum balance enhances our spiritual, mental, emotional and physical health.

Journeying to connect with our Guides is a journey towards wholeness, not only in the psychological sense but also in the sense of knowing our extended selves and developing our potential for awareness. The more whole we can be in ourselves, the clearer, less 'coloured' guidance and teaching are we likely to receive (see also Chapter 8, page 130).

Knowing about chakras enables us to become more conscious of the use of different levels of awareness. A strong root chakra helps to keep us grounded in life and to enhance our ability to accept incarnation, our bodies and the material and sensual worlds. Being grounded is important in order to have easy access to higher levels of awareness, so the routine practice of exercise 1 in Chapter 4, page 55 is vital.

The basic guidance journey (exercise 6, Chapter 5, page 84) and other visual journeys in this book, take you upwards. Although they suggest that you use your heart breath on which to travel into your inner landscape, they invariably take you into the meadow, the place of inner grounding and rooting.

As you journey upwards, you are symbolically journeying through all the layers of your being and harnessing every aspect of yourself to be present for the meeting with your Spirit Guide. The sacral chakra includes in its keywords, power, relationship and creativity. You need all your inner authority to achieve successful channelling communication with your Spirit Guide (see also Chapter 8, page 131). Making a true relationship with your Spirit Guide means that your access to guidance will remain constant and consistent. We have already seen how creativity plays a part in learning to use your inner worlds and contact other dimensions, as discussed in Chapter 5, page 75). Feeding your sacral chakra with its 'home' colour of orange helps in a subtle way to enhance the flow of your creative abilities.

The solar plexus is the centre of identity. In a channelling relationship to a Spirit Guide, as compared with a trance communication, which I consider is now virtually redundant, it is important to maintain your own identity boundaries. The solar plexus is also linked to digestion, to the power of the sun and light and to physical and subtle vision. It helps to provide the energy required for inner journeying and in the symbolic digestion of all that you learn. One of the keywords for the solar plexus is psychic intuition. The word 'psychic' can be used in a number of different ways, and there is a considerable difference between the psychic and the spiritual. Psychological and esoteric languages often use the same words to mean different things. Psychologically speaking 'psychic' refers to that which is 'of the psyche' (see Glossary). It helps to describe the interacting personality and behaviour patterns that make each individual a unique and multi-faceted being.

In esoteric realms the word 'psychic' is used to denote a particular kind of sensitivity. The psychic individual may have premonitions, either in dreams or through 'hunches' and 'knowings'. Crystal ball gazers use the psychic faculty. Tarot card spreads, palm reading, and astrology are becoming re-established as serious studies leading to valuable spiritual and soul guidance. They are also practices that can be energised from a specifically psychic level. The psychic faculty itself is a valuable ingredient in intuition and spiritual practice. However, if it gets stuck at the solar plexus level and isolated there, it becomes limited. Psychic guidance will tend to relate only to the material world, the future, our love lives, 'luck' and all the areas generally associated with 'fortune telling'. Only when integrated with the qualities of the heart and brow chakras does it become truly spiritual.

Psychic energy is responsible for phenomena such as telekinesis, spoon bending, clock stopping, poltergeist happenings and psychometry (the art of attuning to an object in order to find out something about its history or its previous owners). The police sometimes consult mediums with strong psychic faculties in order to find bodies, missing persons or objects.

The psychic world can be both frightening and magical but psychic energy is a necessary ingredient in the vision and power that enables us to see, define, implement and change our spiritual direction. Harnessing the solar plexus ingredient of psychic intuition is important on the journey to being able to work with a Spirit Guide, but it is important to know that over-fascination with this faculty may hinder you in your general spiritual growth and in forming a truly spiritual and mature relationship with your Spirit Guide.

Moving from solar plexus to heart chakra effects a transition that takes you, in terms of levels of awareness, to a place where there is safety from unwanted interference from lower entities, as I discussed in Chapter 5, page 78. The heart is the place where knowledge meets with love and sensitivity and so becomes wisdom. Descartes, the French philosopher, famously said: '*Le coeur a ses raisons que la raison ne connait pas.*' (The heart has a knowledge with which the mind is not acquainted.) In the heart, we evaluate by that which we sense in our inner integrity to be right, rather than through thought and learning. This evaluative level is important to harness in all spiritual growth work.

The throat chakra is connected to the sense of hearing, both physically and symbolically. It is obviously important to keep this activated, alert and healthy when training to receive messages from our Spirit Guides. Also, at the throat chakra, we voice and name things, so bringing them from the abstract into the accessible. This is an important part of our work as channels for Spirit Guides, enabling us to play a part in the complex part of channelling that is about naming and communicating that which they wish to convey.

The rainbow bridge meeting place is on the plateau that is near the top, but not at the top, of a hill or mountain. Knowing that this level represents connection with your brow chakra and the realms of your spirit can help to enhance and focus your ability to reach this level of awareness. Understanding also that the brow chakra connects you to the subtle body known as the higher mental body, as I discuss on page 120, will help you to understand how communication from your Guide becomes manifest for you.

The crown chakra is connected not to Spirit Guides but to the soul and the higher self.

The alter major chakra, which is one of the head chakras and therefore easily connects with your brow charka, helps to put you in touch with instinctual energies and with 'resonance'. The meaning of the word 'resonance' at the alter major chakra is concerned with making links. When your alter major chakra is working well for you, your ability to connect with people – incarnate or discarnate – places or other lifetimes to which you are linked is augmented. Your connection with your power animal is also facilitated by being aware of your alter major chakra, because its element is wet earth and one of its keywords is 'instinct'.

In order to help you to bring all the important energies of the chakra system into your training to work with your Spirit Guide, no formal exercise is necessary. As you read through the attributes and connections of the chakras, you will probably recognise areas in yourself that you feel need further development or attention and be able to relate these to the appropriate chakras. Visualise the home colours of the chakras you want to work with and breathe them in through the chakra petals and out through the stems. Because the alter major chakra has a reversed polarity, you breathe colour in through its stem and out through its petals.

Have some of the crystals relating to the chakras you want to work with in your environment, and hold those of your choice over the petals of the appropriate chakra to help it to be flexible in its natural opening and closing in the course of daily life. Use the fragrances in a burner in your home or added to your bath, or add to a few drops of a carrier oil, such as sweet almond or jojoba oil, to apply directly to your body. If you feel a chakra is too open and vulnerable, use the quietening fragrances. If you feel that the chakra is not open or active enough, use the stimulating oils. If you are pregnant or have allergies or other medical conditions consult a good aromatherapy book or aromatherapist before you use oils extensively. Pure lavender oil is the only one that is safe to apply directly to your skin without carrier oil.

Having looked at the dimension the chakras offer us, it is also useful to know a little more about subtle bodies and the subtle planes to which they can connect us. This will help us in our progression towards communicating with Spirit Guides.

Subtle bodies

In esoteric teachings there are seven layers to our total being and energy field, including the physical body (see diagram on page 104). These subtle bodies link with chakra energies and colours to form layers in our auric field. They also link us in to the subtle layers or other dimensions that interpenetrate with our physical, materially manifest, incarnate, world. Names for the different layers or planes vary throughout esoteric teaching and here I use the terms that Gildas has taught me.

The information given below is mainly included to 'round out' knowledge about your subtle energy field or aura. By doing some basic work with your chakras, as already suggested, you will automatically be strengthening these subtle bodies. By strengthening your subtle bodies you are strengthening the vehicle that makes you receptive to other worlds and enhances the clarity of your perception of them. Cleansing the etheric web, as discussed below, is an important technique to add to your development programme. Paying greater attention to your heart chakra helps your powers of discernment when working in your inner worlds and at the rainbow bridge meeting place.

The etheric body and the etheric web
This is a subtle 'double' of the physical layer and the densest of the subtle bodies. In disease, the etheric body has to repair itself before the physical organs can return to normal. When any part of the

physical body is amputated or removed, its etheric essence remains; the phantom limb is a medically accepted fact.

When the etheric body is 'sensed', it feels tingly, prickly and electric. Its colour is orangey and it has strong links to the sacral chakra and the lymphatic glands. The etheric layer is not so much a plane as a subtle transition area between the physical plane and the astral plane. It is sometimes described as 'the etheric web'. Remnants of every interaction we have 'hang' in the etheric web. If those interactions are bright, celebratory and joyous, then the etheric web of our environment will reflect this, but if there has been sadness, dissention or violence, the subtle 'leftovers' from these will make the etheric web feel heavy.

Cleansing the etheric web

The etheric web around us, therefore, benefits from being 'cleansed'. If it is well cleansed and maintained, then it heightens our vitality and the psychic 'clearness' of our homes.

Gildas suggests that we should routinely imagine ourselves cleansing our own etheric body or web, with a 'toothbrush of light' and also visualise doing this in our homes, especially during and after times of difficulty in our lives.

The astral body and plane

Moving out from the physical body, the second subtle layer or body, known as the astral body, consists of subtle flowing energies. Its colour is yellow gold, rose or a clear, slightly electric, silvery blue. It has strong links to the solar plexus chakra and the adrenal glands. When sensed it feels cool and fluid. The plane of being to which it helps us connect is called 'the astral plane'.

A frequently reported aspect of near-death experience is of being in another part of the room, usually high up near the ceiling, watching what is happening to the physical body. Those who have survived serious accidents have reported watching their physical body being rescued or treated, while their consciousness or essence waits at a distance away from the physical pain and distress. In these experiences the awareness is withdrawn to the astral body or plane.

Many people become attracted to the spiritual path because of the possibility of learning astral travel. In this altered state of consciousness, journeys through time and space and even bi-location become possible. Anyone who wants to work specifically with the esoteric development of the astral body should consult a well-established esoteric school or find a trusted teacher.

The higher astral plane, as described by esotericists, is beautiful. It has flowing landscapes and healing temples. It is the plane where our Spirit Guides, helpers and angels live, move and have their being. When they journey to meet us at our end of the rainbow bridge it is from these planes that they are journeying. When we finally leave our physical bodies, in death, we are guided to this plane by our guardian angels and welcomed there by loved ones, Guides, helpers and angels.

Lower layers of the astral plane are less attractive; thought forms and negative entities populate these regions. Some of the experiences of bad drug trips and schizophrenia can come from a vulnerability that precipitates an unwanted breakthrough into these realms. At the times when we do our practice exercise sessions, work and training to make contact with our Spirit Guides, we need to make sure that our bodies are as clear as possible from over-indulgence of any kind. Because the astral plane has layers, the following planes interact with it and to some degree are enabled by it.

The feeling body and plane
The third subtle layer out from the physical body is termed the 'feeling body'. It has strong links to the heart chakra and the thymus gland. The feeling body is a pale, light green in colour. When sensed it feels warmer, softer and less fluid than the astral body but it is also full of vitality.

When awareness is projected into the feeling body, perceptions are considerably sharpened and heightened. People and objects may be experienced in a special way. Tapping into the feeling body layer enables us to enter a state of contemplation, which is a deep level of meditation. In this state there can be full identification with other people, trees, rocks, plants, crystals or animals. We experience from within, and sense the nature of other beings and life forms, sharing, as much as it is ever possible to share, the nature of other humans or life forms and their rhythms and life cycles. It is the feeling body that enables the ultimate, mystical experience of total oneness or unity with the universe, described by contemplatives, mystics and poets. Those earth-shattering, satisfying moments of unity with a lover, where you lose yourselves in each other, are also an experience enabled by connecting with the feeling body. Because channelling communications from a Spirit Guide eventually requires a degree of merging and blending with their energy or essence, working with your heart chakra, so that your feeling body is energised, is vital to honing the connection.

Using more heart colours – spring green, rose and rose amethyst – in your decor, clothing or environment helps to awaken and open access to your feeling body.

Angelic beings make contact with us from the feeling plane level of the other realms. It is part of the astral plane, but an area in itself.

The mental body and plane

The fourth level out from the physical body is the mental body. When sensed, it has a fluid but tingly texture. It is reflective and glows with subtle shades of blue, silver and turquoise. These are the colours of the throat chakra, to which it has a strong link. The glandular connection is to the thyroid and the parathyroid.

As its name implies, the mental body is partly connected to intellect and abstract thought, to the world of ideas, conceptual blueprints and archetypes as they are manifested. It links us to those unseen patterns, subtle nuances and barely heard sounds, which are aspects of complex communication. It enables us to apprehend, name and implement certain volatile and abstract aspects of the universe and to make use of them in life and incarnation. This includes our integral awareness of, and struggle with, Divine principles or qualities. We feel a true sense of human potential when our societies reflect qualities such as peace, love, justice, respect and a creative relationship to power, and work to achieve interaction with these qualities. Nevertheless we struggle to define these in life. Being in touch with our mental bodies and the mental plane helps us to find integrity.

Divine output flows into the higher mental plane (see brow chakra) but the lower mental plane is where the naming of the things we need to grapple with takes place. Our Spirit Guides have to use our available language and vocabulary, but they are always endeavouring to bring us new concepts and perspectives from the higher mental plane through to the lower mental plane, where we can access them. Communication from a Spirit Guide is a complex process, and having an awareness of our throat chakras and the access this can give to the mental body and the mental plane is a vital part of the process.

The higher mental body
This is the fifth layer working outwards from the physical body. It is linked to the brow chakra and to the pineal gland. The higher mental body is of a supremely light and subtle substance. It reflects deep indigo and amethyst colours and, when sensed, it is filmy, sheer, ethereal, pulsating and cool. The higher mental body is the garment we 'wear' for our highest levels of meditative experience, communication with, and from, other planes and intense moments of inspiration. The mental plane is filled with sheer and pulsating waves. The inspiration that gives birth to ideas originates here, before it becomes clothed with language or form. It is the plane of Divine principle, pure archetypal impulses and of the archangelic beings: Michael, Uriel, Raphael and Gabriel (see Glossary for more detail on pure archetypal impulses and angels). Angels come to the level of our feeling bodies in order to meet us, but their normal 'place of residence' is on the higher mental plane. This is the body we wear when we successfully reach the level of the rainbow bridge. It helps us to be receptive to our Spirit Guides.

The lower causal body

This body does not show as a layer in our auric fields. It is a part of the soul, ketheric or causal body. It is linked to the alter major chakra and to that part of our subtle energy field which governs the rhythms chosen by our souls. Our birth will happen at a specific time and we will be preserved from death until our agreed life span has been reached. Awareness of, and communication with, this layer of our beings brings about a more immediate working out of the karmic laws of cause and effect, leaving less unfinished business to be balanced out in a future lifetime. Connection with Spirit Guides can also have a link to the latter purpose. Knowing our lower causal body through connection with our alter major chakras is therefore important on the journey that leads to working consciously with guidance.

The soul, ketheric or causal body

These are alternative names for the sixth and final subtle body, encountered when moving outwards from the physical body, through the auric field. It is linked to the crown chakra and the pituitary gland. It glows with intense but pale and fine violet light. When sensed, it feels flowing and silky. It has a warm, soft glow.

The ketheric body is an evolutionary imprint or reflection from the soul. In incarnation this layer can affect us through the subtle memories from other lives that cause us to react to positive or nega-tive stimuli in a manner not directly explicable in terms of our present life experience. Unexpectedly intense or so-called irrational fears, 'free floating' anxieties, déjà vu experiences and exceptional giftedness are all examples of the interpenetration of the soul, ketheric or causal body.

The ketheric or causal plane is the area where we are able to consider our past lives and our life plans or purposes for future lives. This plane and the body that links us to it hold the imprint of the learning intentions we have made for this current lifetime. Connecting to this body via our crown chakras will help us to see a higher pattern, purpose and direction in this life and to remember the times when we and our Spirit Guides have met before.

It is possible to use this basic knowledge of chakras, subtle bodies and planes to amplify your ability to focus at the level of the rainbow bridge.

Exercise 7: *Using chakras to focus at the rainbow bridge level of awareness*

This exercise will also be useful to those who find visual guided journeys difficult to sustain. Although it refers only to chakras and not to subtle bodies, remember that work with your chakras is *also* work for your subtle bodies and for your perception of subtle planes. Make the general preparations as described in Chapter 4, page 54, and then do exercise 1, Chapter 4, page 55.

1. After the grounding exercise, endeavour to locate your seven major chakras in relationship to your physical body.

2. Start at the root chakra and sense the area of its energy; breathe into that area. Work upwards, in your own time, sensing each chakra, breathing into it and thinking of its main colour. So, when you are at your root chakra, think red, think orange at your sacral chakra, yellow at your solar plexus, spring green at your heart, lapis lazuli blue at your throat, indigo at your brow and violet at your crown. Just thinking about these colours is enough, you do not have to visualise them vividly.

3. Having located each chakra area and breathed into it, return to focus your awareness at your root chakra. Breathe into it, using your breath to help you focus on this area for a few moments.

4. Breathe up from your root chakra to your sacral chakra and repeat this six times. Focus your breathing on your sacral chakra for a few moments.

5. Breathe up from your sacral chakra to your solar plexus chakra, repeating the upward breath six times; thereafter focusing on your solar plexus chakra by breathing gently into it for a few moments.

6. Breathe up from your solar plexus chakra to your heart chakra, repeating the upward breath six times; thereafter focusing on your heart chakra by breathing gently into it for a few moments.

7. Breathe up from your heart chakra to your throat chakra, repeating the upward breath six times; thereafter focusing on your throat chakra by breathing gently into it for a few moments.

8. Breathe up from your throat chakra to your brow chakra, repeating the upward breath six times; thereafter focusing on your brow chakra by breathing into it and aiming to maintain your focus at this level for at least ten minutes.

9. You can use this exercise as a discipline and focusing exercise to reach the rainbow bridge level of awareness. You do not need to visualise the rainbow bridge.

10. After ten minutes, return to an awareness of your body and your outer surroundings and put a cloak of light with a hood right around you, and be aware of your feet in contact with the ground.

11. Make notes in your special book before resuming your normal activities.

Alternatively you can use this exercise to reach the right level for receiving guidance:

1. Having reached the brow chakra level and focused on it for a few moments, invoke the presence of your Spirit Guide and hold any questions you may have requiring guidance in the focus of your regular breathing into your brow chakra.

2. When you are ready, or after no more than 20 minutes, return to your awareness of your body and your outer surroundings. Put the cloak of light with a hood right around you and be aware of your feet in contact with the ground, before making notes in your special book and resuming your normal activities.

Chapter 8 looks beyond the stage where you receive simple messages, knowings or symbolic guidance, to the area of receiving substantial channelling on a regular basis and with an assured contact and connection with your Spirit Guide.

8

Towards a Fuller Relationship with your Spirit Guide

This chapter looks firstly at the implications of the move from the astrological age of Pisces to the astrological age of Aquarius, which took place at the millennium. With this astrological move, the role of the channeller of Spirit Guidance is also changing. We have to take on more responsibility for what is channelled and the way in which it is channelled. If full-trance mediumship is largely a thing of the past, as I believe it to be, then, for the aspiring channeller, work on the self is important.

The preparation required to be a reliable and coherent channel is not about learning how to make large shifts into dramatically altered states of awareness but more about self-knowledge and individual vulnerability. This chapter looks at ways of working on yourself so that you learn to be more 'transparent' and thus can avoid the main traps of 'colouring' in guidance as much as possible.

The ages of Pisces and Aquarius

We are at the beginning of a new millennium, which means that astrologically we have moved into the influence of a new sign. This happens at a collective level only once every 2,000 years. We have recently left the age of Pisces in order to arrive in the age of Aquarius – we cannot escape change. It is at such times of significant collective and individual change that Spirit Guides, whose work is to help humanity to reach its full potential, become particularly active in endeavouring to reach, teach and encourage us. We live in exciting but confusing times.

The point at which one astrological sign changes to another is known as 'the cusp'. In the normal astrological year, where the signs change monthly, the cusp may last for a day or so, but in the greater 2,000-year cycles it is proportionately longer. Although it is difficult to calculate precisely, most astrologers felt that the influence of Aquarius became active just before the millennium, but the changeover would remain cuspal for some ten years or so after the turn of the millennium.

The cuspal point – as the retreating influence gives way to the one that is emerging – can be tricky. Uncertainties, insecurities and the breakdown of old systems are inevitable. Even favourable change and the positive opportunities that emerge can be unsettling and demanding. At the beginning of the new millennium the retreat of Pisces and the emergence of Aquarius are presenting challenges to humanity and the planet. The need of our Spirit Guides to be more active at such a time affects the fields of mediumship, channelling and spiritual growth.

Pisces is a water sign: its glyph or symbol shows two fish swimming in opposite directions to form a circle. Spiritually, Pisces makes us flow towards the saviour, guru or parent/redeemer. It leads us to understand the nature of sacrifice but tends to fix us in the role of the disciple, devotee, pupil or spiritual child. Although it inspires the collective search for spiritual truth, it also leads us into the dogmatic jungle. At an individual level it fosters dependency and a slavish obedience to authority.

Aquarius, despite its glyph/symbol of the water carrier, is an air sign. It urges us to individuality and encourages the finding of our own *inner* wisdom and authority. It makes us question outer authority and known patterns with a healthy cynicism. In the years of the first flush of its influence, the sign of Aquarius will tend to highlight our need for self-development and self-responsibility. It will tend to lead to difficulties in community life, families, partnerships and all joint ventures. As this cuspal phase of assertion comes to an end we will be more mutually tolerant and respectful, honouring, valuing and even able to celebrate each other's differences. This will enable the development of spiritually and emotionally mature relation-ships, systems of government, community dynamics and world peace.

These changes deeply affect the guidance scene and especially those who want to have a deep and consistent relationship with a Spirit Guide. The Piscean medium could often be a passive channel with little required other than a natural gift for openness to other worlds and the beings who inhabit them. The age of Pisces was the age of the full-trance medium who would often allow another entity to enter and take over their physical body completely for a prescribed period of time. It was the age of psychic phenomena, when many marvels undoubtedly happened but when deliberate fraudulent fakings were also exposed. These exposures affected the integrity and reputation of the whole world of mediumship and communication with other dimensions.

The Aquarian model of relating to other worlds and entities, however, opens up new perspectives and brings new challenges. The Aquarian channel, to whom this book aims to speak, will rarely enter full trance. A lightly altered state of consciousness is sufficient. Dramatic psychic phenomena have become less valued and therefore less sought after. It is easy to be self-deluding; but where drama is less to the fore, deliberate fraud can become a thing of the past.

The Aquarian change in relationship with a Spirit Guide is largely one instigated by the Guides themselves. It is a conscious and co-operative relationship; indeed, one of Gildas's most frequently used words is 'co-creativity'. The channel is no longer permitted to be passive/receptive but needs to be active/receptive and co-creative. This puts some extra responsibilities on to the channel in terms of psychological clearance and self-growth, but it helps us to move ourselves on, as the age of Aquarius demands, into a different rela-tionship to authority. Most Spirit Guides want to be friends, advisers, teachers and healers, telling us about our potential and how we *can* live through our own choices, not through authorities telling us *how* we must live.

The step into more serious channelling

There is no doubt in my mind that knowing you have a Guide who is there for you and being able to ask for help and support at times of stress and choice is a potential life-opening and enhancement factor. You can use the information and the exercises in this book to develop a Spirit Guide awareness that is full of light and delight – and that may be all that you seek and need.

This kind of relationship enables you to be aware of another dimension, to set your life in a wider context and to have a clearer consciousness about any life choices you need to make. It may enable you to share guidance experiences with other friends or in groups and to develop the ability to offer channelled guidance to those around you who are experiencing dilemmas of choice. Working to have this kind of contact with a Guide is a whole area of spiritual growth and expansion in itself.

Going further

If, however, you feel that you want to channel more substantial teachings and enter into philosophical discussion with your Spirit Guide, and to use guidance on a wider, more formal or consistent basis then attention to your own psychological and spiritual growth is essential. You may want to channel significant help for yourself and others for their dilemmas, spiritual growth and teaching about other worlds, or you may want to have a healing Guide alongside you to enhance and complement your own gifts as a healer. If this is the case, you need to pay more specific attention to clearing yourself to become a clear and co-creative channel.

All the information in this book about other worlds and the philo-sophical basis from which our Spirit Guides bring their wisdom has originally been channelled from my connection with Gildas. He continues to give expansive and thought-provoking teachings in my monthly groups after over 45 years of constant communication. I am the co-creative channel for this, in that I cooperate with the opportunity for it to happen.

Over the years I have built up a 'spiritual vocabulary' to make it easier for Gildas to communicate new concepts or spiritual approaches, but I rarely read spiritual books. The reason for this is that with the volume of work I do with Gildas, I am wary of the phenomenon of 'colouring', as I discuss on page 130. Our most co-creative work comes mainly with healing and in the design of workshops and spiritual growth exercises. Gildas supports and inspires me as a healer and helps to enhance my sensitivity. I use my psychotherapeutic and counselling skills to help people explore their relationship to their illnesses (see also Further Reading, my book *Energy Healing for Beginners*). When designing workshops and spiritual growth exercises, Gildas again provides inspiration, ideas and concepts, but my trained knowledge is called upon in helping to make the exercises safe and in adopting/applying/relating the appropriate relationship to the field of psychology.

From the time when my spiritual worlds and awareness of Gildas caused me such inner confusion that my physical eyesight was affected for a while, as explained in the Introduction, I knew that a pathway of self-growth and the need for psychological help along the way was going to be inevitable. From the age of 19 this help was always synchronistically available. I know that many of those people who currently use their channelling gifts substantially and professionally have similar stories to tell. If life is carrying you along into this sort of development you will inevitably know about it, but there is a line between the satisfactory and satisfying albeit lighter contact with your Spirit Guide and the practice of full professional channelling, which you might become eager to pursue. The following issues and exercises will benefit you whatever place you want your Spirit Guide to take in your life, but they are essential if you want to develop a more sustained and serious type of channelling, especially if it is for the guidance of others. The spiritual and personal growth that can come from working with the issues considered in this chapter and from following exercise 8 onwards will help you to become a clearer channel. I would also recommend that you read and consider this chapter before consulting a channel or medium or before reading any of the substantial volume of channelled material that is now available on the Internet and elsewhere.

The phenomenon of colouring

Awareness of colouring will prevent you from giving the contents of channelled messages too much authority without due consideration, as well as alerting you to the need for interpretation and to make you more thoughtful about the whole nature of Spirit Guides and the processes of channelling and guidance.

Although the Aquarian model of channelling is one that I find exciting and expansive, without full trance the channel's own belief systems, authority hang-ups, limitations in vocabulary, imperfect attunement and emotional attachment to the results can all colour and affect the messages that come through. Continuing with full-trance mediumship is out of the question, the times in which we live require this conscious cooperative and co-creative interaction between the worlds and dimensions, even though, or perhaps especially because, this also tends to throw us back on ourselves and makes us face our many-faceted inadequacies.

In this new model of channelling we will hear only what we are capable of hearing. Unless we work to clear ourselves of conditioning and hang-ups, particularly around authority issues, we will perpetuate the saviour/disciple, guru/devotee, teacher/pupil and parent/redeemer/child archetypes well beyond their sell-by dates.

People who have started to receive messages from their Spirit Guides often complain that it is difficult to get clear or definitive guidance for themselves and those very close to them. Indeed it is! When I attune to Gildas to receive his comments on the problems of those who come to consult us, I know that I can stay detached from what those comments may be. The dilemmas that come into my workroom move me, activate my compassion, have me open-mouthed at the courageous ways in which people manage their lives and the burdens they have to bear, but I don't have any real difficulty in getting myself out of the way so that Gildas's perspective on the questions asked can be as clearly channelled as possible.

However, when it comes to asking for his perspective for myself, it is a different matter: if I hear what I want to hear, I suspect that I may have coloured the responses, and, equally, if I hear what I don't particularly want to hear or look at, I wonder if my inner saboteur is raising its ugly head again. I also fear that when channelling for close and loved ones, what *I* want for them may slip through. On the occasions when I have been persuaded to ask for advice for them I have had first to work hard to make conscious any emotional investment I may have.

Spirit Guides have their own particular characteristics. However, if you receive guidance from a Guide who appears to have an 'axe to grind', take a closer look at the channel, or yourself, if you are the channel. Do they or you have too much reverence for exacting or disciplining authority? Or too little? Do you or they have a tendency to be judgemental, too conservative or too liberal? Do you or they sit on the fence and fear commitment? Are you or they capable of clear, detached thinking? If Guides consistently have a tendency to echo any extremism in the channel, colouring is probably present. Because none of us can ever claim to be completely unbiased or detached, we must assume that some colouring is always present. It is the degree of its influence that is important. Applying these questions to yourself as a channel and attempting to give honest answers without either false pride or false modesty will show you the areas you need to work on within yourself to clear the way for reliable and substantial guidance to be channelled through you.

Colouring of this kind means that it is necessary to be aware of the need to make allowances. Never follow guidance blindly. Always stop to think whether any advice on which you plan to act is in tune with your own intuition and integrity. It is surprising how many seemingly sane, balanced and wise people will suddenly do things entirely out of character or for glaringly ill-advised reasons just because a discarnate entity, with doubtful credentials, channelled through a fallible human being, has said so.

From time to time wise Guides, channelled at a particularly high level, may urge you to take calculated risks. If these are in line with your creative vision and are the prompt or permission you needed, then your life may change for the better as a result. If such suggestions are ungrounded in reality or are made without due regard for current responsibilities, then acting on them without also giving credence to your own inner wisdom or gut feeling may mean that some hard lessons are learned.

Our true Spirit Guides are rarely stern, dogmatic, domineering, peremptory or over-directive. The case of false guidance – Amanda's story, quoted in Chapter 3, page 42 – was in the tone of: 'You've got everything wrong. You have made a mess of your life. Pack your bags today and go to Australia. If you do not do this there will be no more help.'

Even when making allowances for colouring, this is not the voice of a true, higher Spirit Guide. Imagine that you are in a desperate situation and that you have come for guidance as a last resort. You are feeling a failure. You are blaming yourself. You are full of guilt. You then receive a peremptory directive to which, you are warned, failure to obey will result in being cut off from spiritual help and support. The effects of such a message could be dangerous and devastating. Part of the responsibility of the cooperative and co-creative channelling of the Aquarian age is for the channel to do everything possible to endeavour to ensure that such messages do not get through.

A more positive aspect of colouring is that which gives a particular Guide special characteristics. All true Spirit Guides have a great sense of humour. Many adopt certain phrases and tones or subtly manifest traits and a style that makes them particularly identifiable. Gildas is gentle. He is often a master of understatement. When he knows a group or individual to have lost any first awe of him, he will gently tease or make humorous comments about the group process, the individual and things happening in the immediate outer environment.

Other Guides are known for their energy and inspire their channels to make wide gestures or challenge their audiences in order to provoke discussion or thought.

It is important that characteristics that belong to specific Guides are those of the Guide and not those of the channel. Unless the channel is 'transparent' then issues the channel has at a personal level will colour the way in which the Spirit Guide is presented.

Authority issues and conditioning

Throughout our lives we feel constrained to please others. Parents, teachers, society, eventually even parts of our inner selves, all demand some form of obedience or conformity. Compliance is the norm. We expect to be given examples and precepts on which to model ourselves.

Few of us are completely pleased with our lives. When we become parents, we try to prevent our children from making the mistakes we feel we have made. We push our children to achieve where we failed and to become that which we longed to be. We look at society and try to groom our offspring to fit the roles which society demands or rewards the most. We forget that we probably learned little from our parents' mistakes. Children, from birth, are distinct individuals with their own blueprints. We give the best upbringing when we are constantly alert to find what the blueprint may be and to encourage and nurture it.

The dissatisfactions we have with our own lives are largely due to seeking approval, living out others' expectations and succumbing to conditioning that is not fully in tune with our true selves. When we have children of our own, we tend, almost robotically, to be guilty of perpetuating the same system. With horror we hear coming out of our own mouths, to our own children, the very statements which made us squirm when our own parents said them to us: 'I had to conform to my parents'/teachers' wishes and it never did *me* any harm'; 'I went to a strictly disciplinarian school and learned to toe the line – it wasn't such a bad thing.' If we carefully consider such statements we may realise the hurt or wounding that underlies them. Sometimes the fear of facing that pain is the cause of our sustaining the very structures we inwardly despise.

Although some conformity is necessary to the smooth running of society, blind, unquestioning obedience is dangerous. It encourages politics of power rather than ensuring caring government and nurturing individual talents. If we conform or obey without question we hand over self-responsibility and deny ourselves choices. We sit back and blame the authorities – the all-powerful 'they' – without recourse to our rights to have a say in who 'they' are and how 'they' should act. We create hierarchies, expect to look up to our leaders and feel betrayed by them when they fail to meet our expectations. We must be wary of putting this kind of authority and expectation on to either our Spirit Guides or those who channel them.

One way of exploring our own vulnerabilities and areas where we might be likely to colour the guidance channelled through us is to work with subpersonalities. It is psychological work that we can safely do without specific counselling or psychotherapeutic support. As we work with our subpersonalities so we help ourselves to achieve the transparency that makes us clear channels.

Subpersonalities

When entering any growth process involving self-knowledge, inevitably we become aware of the complexity of our inner psychological mechanisms. What, for instance, lies behind the use of the pronoun 'I'? 'I am a woman/man', 'I like swimming', 'I am a teacher', 'I am married/single', and so on? We might also say: 'Part of me wants to go swimming and part of me doesn't', 'Part of me likes tidiness but another part is just a muddler', 'Sometimes when I want to have fun, part of me holds back', 'I am very hard on myself', 'My spiteful, jealous side sometimes betrays me', 'How could I have behaved like that and said those rude things at that time?'

Usually when we say 'I', the part we know, trust and with which we identify is speaking. When we explore ourselves further we might find, either to our delight or consternation, that we are legion.

The Italian psychologist Roberto Assagioli formulated the system of self-analysis known as psychosynthesis (see Further Reading). He named the different aspects of ourselves 'subpersonalities'. Earlier, C. G. Jung had spoken of the 'persona' or 'mask'. Our working and professional selves or personas are often quite different from our relaxed, private or holiday selves. We, and those with whom we live and work, need these masks, which help us to play the many differ-ent roles life demands of us. We even wear certain uniforms to help the persona to operate. The pin-striped suit for business, the apron for housework, the sporting gear for jogging, the T-shirt for relax-ation, the formal or beautiful clothes for entertaining and party-going are all supports for essential aspects of our day-to-day interactions.

In some ways the concept of the subpersonality goes further than that of the persona and refers to the deeper dynamics at work within the psyche. We use the persona more consciously. The subpersonal-ities develop as a result of conditioning and can be survival mechanisms. They are distinctive energies within the psyche.

In order to deal with the kind of conditioning that crushes our true, or core, selves, we inwardly create subpersonalities to help us make the outwardly required 'grade', but, although they are survival mechanisms, they often mask our true selves until we name, recog-nise and work with them. Subpersonalities usually develop and manifest as pairs of opposites. Therefore, if we have been required in childhood to be over-orderly, we may develop an obsessively tidy subpersonality but also one which is disordered and chaotic. If we have been subject to power and manipulation there may be an inner tyrant and an inner victim. Where it was demanded that we become too 'good' we might have an inner 'goody-goody' or strict moralist but also a naughty, devious, dishonest or sly subpersonality.

These pairs perpetuate each other, and until you work with them they will remain largely in your unconscious mind where they may become autonomous and somewhat dissociated. They may emerge to embarrass and surprise us in unexpected situations, particularly when we are under stress. Our friends may remark: 'I've never really seen that side of you before. Your behaviour at that party/meeting/encounter was quite a revelation.'

Fortunately subpersonalities are extremely rewarding to work with. They reveal themselves readily when we seek them out. When they tell their stories and help us to understand what they see and why they have developed, they can become important allies in the journey to self-knowledge. Exercise 8 at the end of this chapter will help you to meet some of yours.

Knowing our subpersonalities gives us insight into the vulnerable areas of our make-up, which may cause colouring in the channelling we receive from our Spirit Guides and create obstacles on the way to clarity. Armed with this knowledge we are also better able, where necessary, to evaluate and interpret any guidance we have sought. So, on the journey to serious contact with our Spirit Guides, taking time to know your subpersonalities can be of great benefit.

The exercise below gives you a way of getting to know your subpersonalities and of being able to work with them on a more extended basis. Such work will help you develop your emotional maturity and emotional intelligence. Taking this kind of journey also helps you to be more 'at home' in your own inner worlds and landscape and to have greater access to inner resources.

Working with subpersonalities

In Chapter 4, exercise 3, page 58, you found a journey to meet your inner wise being or presence, and subsequent exercises suggested that you take with you this aspect of your inner wisdom. It is possible for the unconscious or semi-conscious presence of troublesome subpersonalities to block or mask clear access to our inner wise beings. As we work with the subpersonalities the connections to wisdom will improve. Yet because the inner wise being is always somewhere within our make-up, it is advisable to use the following exercise to connect with its presence as a first part to the subpersonality exercise. The inner wise being can then witness the exploration of our subpersonalities, both protecting us and growing stronger in itself throughout the process. In exercise 8, the journey to meet your inner wise presence is repeated to enable you to avoid having to go back to exercise 3, Chapter 4.

Exercise 8: *Guided journey to your inner wise being and subpersonalities*

Subpersonalities can appear in a multitude of forms: as stereotyped people, as animals, birds, and mythical creatures or as cartoon characters with a twist of humour in the way in which they present themselves. One client had a 'Chewing Gum Wizard' who was something of a shape shifter. Sometimes they manifest as an inseparable pair, such as twins, even conjoined twins, or as animated objects; Joanna had a troublesome victim/tyrant pair of subpersonalities who appeared as a bat and ball (see Joanna's story, page 141). Usually subpersonalities communicate willingly, clearly telling their stories and what they may require of us. They will also, with our help, communicate with each other. Eventually they may outlive their purpose and fade away, they may change or transform into valued inner allies or they may merge and blend with each other, making our inner family a less numerous or unwieldy bunch.

Before you start the exercise, make the initial preparations suggested before exercise 1, Chapter 4, page 54.

1. Become aware of the rhythm of your breathing and bring that rhythm into your heart centre or chakra, thus activating your heart energy on which to travel into your

inner landscape. Find yourself in a meadow and take the opportunity to activate all your inner senses so that you see the objects and colours, hear the sounds, touch the textures, smell the fragrances and savour the tastes.

2. Be aware of your inner landscape around and beyond your meadow. Know that somewhere in this landscape your inner wise presence dwells. Call this being or presence to be with you, now in your meadow, ready to accompany you on your journey to the houseboat, on the river of life where your subpersonalities live. You might also like to ask your power animal to accompany you now and to make sure that you have with you any special talisman or amulet you like to take on inner journeys.

3. This next part of the journey gives you the opportunity to meet no more than four subpersonalities who may have a bearing on your search for clear contact with, and channelling of, your Spirit Guide.

4. Somewhere in your inner landscape, maybe quite close to the meadow, there is a river and you now journey to this river, with your companions.

5. As you walk beside the river you will become aware that nearby there is a quiet stretch of backwater or tributary stream. Anchored on this backwater or stream is a houseboat which is where your subpersonalities live.

6. As you draw near to the boat you may be aware of the activity and noise of your subpersonalities as they live out their lives on board.

7. Stand back and observe the boat. What sort of boat is it? What is its state of repair and upkeep? What are the arrangements for boarding and landing?

8. After this initial inspection, withdraw a little from the water's edge and find a comfortable place in which to sit, whilst keeping the boat in full view. Choose a sun-warmed rock and rest your back against it. Be aware of your inner wise presence and perhaps your power animal supporting you.

9. Ask that no more than four of your subpersonalities from the houseboat prepare to reveal themselves to you. On this occasion, invite out only those subpersonalities who might in any way be blocking your ability to work clearly with your Spirit Guide or who might be likely to colour the quality and content of any communications you are likely to receive.

10. Insist that the subpersonalities reveal themselves to you one at a time, unless they are component parts of a pair, like twins. When you have met and greeted the first it should step to one side as you greet the next. The second should then step back as you greet the third and the third should make way, in its turn, for the fourth.

11. Observe and greet each subpersonality and let them also observe and greet you. Ask each one to tell you their story in brief (how and when they came into being, what they fear and what they require at this time, and so on).

12. When you have met these subpersonalities, reflect whether any two of them might benefit from talking to each other in your presence and that of your inner wise being. Ask your inner wise being for advice on this. Do not put this

dialogue into effect on this occasion, merely become aware of what might be of value.

13. Before asking your subpersonalities to return to the houseboat consider whether you are ready to make any commitment to work with them further.

14. Thank your subpersonalities for revealing themselves and ask them to return to the houseboat, giving them any reassurances or promises of further work, if you feel that you want to and are able to pursue this.

15. When the subpersonalities are safely aboard, journey back to your meadow, accompanied by your inner wise presence and your power animal.

16. From the meadow return to the rhythm of your breathing in your heart centre, to your awareness of your body, your contact with the ground and your normal surroundings. Imagine that there is a cloak of light with a hood right around you.

17. Take time to record your journey in your special book.

Once you have established this journey to the place in your inner landscape where your subpersonalities live, you can return for further work with them. You may have felt that two or more of them should communicate together, or that you need to talk more seriously with one or more of them about their present needs and natures. You may want to agree with a subpersonality that you will give it something it needs in return for it giving something to you. This giving and receiving may be in the form of symbolic gifts, but it may also mean that you make something the subpersonality has to offer into more of an ally in your life, in return for it giving you more self-assurance because you know it will no longer pop out inappropriately. Use your creativity and your growing understanding of these mechanisms to find ways of modifying their weaknesses and autonomy or harnessing their strengths. Do not commit yourself to anything you will be unable to carry out in the near future. Try to keep a record of all this inner work on yourself and your identity in your special book.

Joanna's story: the bat and ball subpersonality
A group on a course of workshops for the development of contact with Spirit Guides and channelling included Joanna. She greatly enjoyed the work and quite quickly felt that she was in good contact with her male Spirit Guide from whom she received images and short phrases in response to the questions and information she asked of him. However, she was unsettled about the way that I would banter with my own Spirit Guide, Gildas.

As Gildas felt the group getting more comfortable with him he began to exhibit some of his humour and more informal teasing traits, as I communicated with him for the group. When talking to the group about him after such a session, I was sometimes decidedly irreverent in a bantering kind of way, which marks one of the qualities of our long relationship.

I felt sometimes that Joanna was not entirely comfortable with this kind of interaction, so I took the opportunity to explain that playfulness with our Spirit Guides helps us to relax and be creative with them. Talking individually with her, she expressed fears that if we lost a sense of awe for our Guides and tried too much for the lighter side of the relationship, we might colour what they have to teach and prevent it from being serious enough.

I reiterated for her that every relationship between a human being and their Spirit Guide is different and that, having been channelling Gildas's communications for over 45 years, I felt comfortable enough with him to banter with him sometimes. I explained that this had increased my respect for the work and the quality of my relationship with him, rather than diminished it. I also told her that over the past few years, since our relationship has become even more relaxed, I felt that the communications from Gildas had deepened and in many ways were more awe-inspiring than ever. I suggested, also, that perhaps her sense of wanting to keep her relationship with her Spirit Guide on a very formal level might be one of the factors making it difficult for her to reach the stage of a more sustained and coherent flow of information from him.

When the group performed the subpersonality exercise given on page 137, one of Joanna's subpersonalities was represented by a bat and ball. But, far from having fun together, the bat was 'out to get' the ball and chased and pushed and flung it everywhere, leaving the ball no hiding place. It was even quite difficult to get them to stay quiet for long enough to tell the story of how they had come into being. They eventually said that they had developed during an era in Joanna's life when, aged six years, she had gone to stay with a great aunt for an extended period because her mother had pregnancy complications before the birth of Joanna's brother.

It was an emotional story that Joanna courageously shared with her small group after the exercise. Having been an only child for six years and rarely staying away from home without one or other of her parents also being present, going away to stay alone with her aunt, whom she hardly knew, was a traumatic experience. She sensed that there was something desperately wrong with her mother, but because the pregnancy had such complications and her mother had to be hospitalised for the final four months, her parents had not told her that a new baby might be coming. She learned, much later, that both the life of her mother and the child she was carrying were at serious risk. Her father had been frantic and simply could not cope with his wife in hospital and in danger and the threatened loss of a much-wanted second child as well as work and caring for Joanna.

The childless great aunt had offered her services, but the whole episode had not been thought through. Great Aunt Beatrice lived so far away from Joanna's home that her father could only make rare visits during the time she was there. Joanna felt exiled, abandoned and confused. Great Aunt Beatrice was not used to children and felt that Joanna should mainly speak only when spoken to. Joanna became lonely and bored, away from her friends and with little to do, with a woman who meant well but had no experience of young children. Recognising that her great niece was bored, Great Aunt Beatrice found all kinds of jobs in the home for her to do and even made out rotas for her, which listed how her time should be divided between one job and another.

As the period of staying with her great aunt was extended, Joanna had, briefly, gone to a school in the area, but had made no friends and felt even more strange and abandoned because of this arrangement.

Eventually the time came when the announcement was made that Joanna now had a new brother and could return home. Her father would be coming to fetch her the next day. Joanna said she felt confused rather than excited and consciously wondered that if this baby was now in her home could it mean that she was no longer welcome or that she would no longer be a permanent resident with her parents? She had taken a doll with her to her aunt's and had found it a great source of comfort during this bleak time. She felt it was enormously significant that on the journey home with her father she realised her favourite toy had been left behind when it was too late to go back. Joanna said: 'It was a doll that was like a real baby. I suppose I wanted to leave the new baby behind and all the experiences that had gone with his birth, but I also feel now that I had left my childhood behind at that moment.'

When she got home, Joanna's mother was still not well and, although she welcomed Joanna and tried to give her a lot of extra attention, her energy was limited and the new baby brother was demanding. For the best reasons, Joanna's mother tried to involve her in the care of her brother. This was fun at first but gradually she was relied on for baby care in a way that was too much for a six-year-old. After her traumatic pregnancy Joanna's mother was never really relaxed, energetic or fun-loving again and Joanna felt she ran about all the time doing too many of the jobs her mother had not had enough energy to do.

Considering the bat and ball subpersonality, Joanna felt that she was the ball and that life was the bat. She had a strong inner message that she was only here to serve and that if ever she tried to be in her own space, something or someone would come to get her out. She said that her present boss at work was a bit like a bat, too: driving and pursuing, over-demanding and controlling of his staff.

The bat and ball subpersonality made it obvious why Joanna had problems with play, light-heartedness and authority. Her early close, only child relationship with her parents had been betrayed. She had had to grow up too soon. It was dangerous to get close or relax, because you might be batted off to an uncomfortable place. She carried an inner message that she was here only to serve and it was easy for her to become the victim whenever there was a potential tyrant around.

Joanna realised that a bat and ball are originally for play and they eventually told her that they longed to learn to play again so that the bat could send the ball off playfully and the ball would not feel the need to try to hide, but would bounce back with joy, asking for more.

Looking at how this subpersonality affected her relationship with her Spirit Guide, Joanna realised that every time she felt the connection was close enough for the longed-for flow to happen, she felt anxious and, without waiting to be 'batted', she autonomously bounced away.

There was much to work on here. The apparently light-hearted symbolism of bat and ball actually carried a lot of heavy material. Making it conscious, however, helped Joanna to see where she needed to change in her attitude and negative expectations, not only in relationship to her Spirit Guide but in the whole of life itself.

It was a moving and joyful moment when, as a presage to one of the longer communications Joanna had longed for, her Spirit Guide said gently, 'Joanna, remember that I am not the tyrant bat who is a threat to your victim ball, but I long to play a more joyous game of bat and ball as we learn to dialogue with each other in a lively manner.'

*   *   *

At this stage, you have eight exercises that, regularly practised, will help you to develop a reliable contact with your Spirit Guide. So now you might well be asking the question: 'Where do I go from here?' The next chapter gives exercises for developing and maintaining contact with your Spirit Guide as well as considering the uses to which you might want to put your ability to work with them. It also gives advice and exercises for maintaining your auric health and vitality so that moving between the connection with other dimensions and everyday living becomes ever smoother and can be embraced easily as a part of the whole of your life.

9

Developing and Maintaining your Spirit Guide Contact

One of the fascinating things about working with Spirit Guides is that there is always something new to learn or to develop. By using and reusing the exercises and information given so far in this book you will reach a level of connection with your Guide that is right for you. Yet, you will still have many questions you will wish to find answers for.

As your Guide becomes an ever-more familiar friend and mentor, so he or she is likely to take over your further training. But until that happens, and on the way to it happening, this last chapter will give you some final suggestions on how to enrich what you have already learned and how to move forward.

In your further work you may want to know more about psychic protection and so I have covered this later in the chapter. You may also be curious to discover where you might have met your Guide before. Exercise 10 on page 157 will help you to learn this, and it will also place your guidance work in the context of your personal evolution and what your higher self may be wanting you to build on from things you have known and contacts you have made in previous lifetimes, as I discussed in Chapter 2.

Further development for the guidance connection

The exercises in this book are designed to be practised many times, with perseverance. This should continue until you are aware, even if only to a slight degree, that when you go to the meeting place you are not alone: although you might not see your Spirit Guide in full costume or regalia, you will have received signs (see Chapter 5, page 79), heard a voice or received communication in any of the ways outlined in Chapter 6.

In Chapter 5, page 70 I suggested 'acting as if' as a valid way to enhance the possibility of meeting your Spirit Guide. Once you regularly have the sense that when you go to the rainbow bridge meeting place you are not alone, it is important to intensify this 'acting as if'. In this way you honour the presence of your Spirit Guide and make more and more opportunities for you to pick up on that subtle change of vibration that is your Guide's way of reassuring you that he or she is near and moving into closer connection with your energy field. Remember, everyone *has* a Spirit Guide and although not everyone has a strong connection with this world of guidance, these shining beings are with us always and they endeavour to help and guide us at every bend or undulation of our life's path. Picking up the vibrational change that assures us of their presence is a matter of continually training our sensitivity and perception and letting go of rigid expectations.

Whenever possible, try to keep a notepad with you so that you can jot down those moments when you feel an unexpected idea or thought come into your head. Eventually, you may begin to sense the subtle nuance that tells you it is about to happen, just before it does. This may then lead to being able to 'shift your level of awareness' quite quickly if the circumstances are right, so that you can experience a more defined connection with your Guide.

The journey to the rainbow bridge will always be the principal way in which to have a meeting with our Guides and to enable the links required for strong communicative contact to develop. But relaxation and play are also important factors in building a creative relationship to our Spirit Guides. Exercise 9 on page 155 takes you on a journey to provide yourself with a place where you might invite your Guide to come and be with you in more relaxed mood.

Vocabulary

In conscious co-creative channelling or mediumship, the Guide can use only the vocabulary of the channel. Words that are rarely used ordinarily by the channel will be used in different ways and contexts, there will be different turns of phrase and the Guide will coin characteristic expressions – but the words used are all within the channeller's knowledge. If specialist information is required, using a specific vocabulary unfamiliar to the channel, then that information can come through only if the channel learns or is exposed to that vocabulary.

Speeding up the contact process

If you are new to this work, it is essential to practise the basic exercise for journeying to the meeting place with your Guide for a considerable period of time. You can practise either the visual, guided journey, given in exercise 3, Chapter 4, page 58 or the exercise which uses the chakras to focus at the rainbow bridge level of awareness given in exercise 7, Chapter 7, page 122. Careful attention to the details and sequences ensures your safety and also trains you to focus your awareness at different levels.

With practice, however, there will come a time when you can speed up the process and travel in a very short time indeed from heart breath, to meadow, to harnessing the inner senses, to being joined by your power animal and inner wise presence or being and, finally, to reaching the plateau. You can learn to 'see' the whole scenario in moments and to achieve an efficient shift in level. This speed can be achieved using both methods mentioned above. You will also gradually and naturally be able to increase the speed it takes to 'come back', but never underestimate this. Be certain that you can become quickly and totally focused in the outer world, quite naturally. Always make sure that you have connected with the earth beneath your feet and know exactly what you are going to do next. This is particularly important if you are going to do other outer-world tasks immediately; for example, if you are going to meet other people who have not been where you have been, or are about to make a journey, especially if you will be driving a car.

When I lead channelling courses, and channel Gildas for the participants, the question is often asked: 'Do you still do the whole guidance journey from heart breath to rainbow bridge?' On most occasions I do indeed, but very quickly. On other occasions I use the benefit of now knowing the energy line and vibration on which I connect with Gildas so well that, rather like making a telephone call, I can 'dial up' and be in contact almost instantly. As I do not register all that Gildas says when he is speaking to individuals or groups, I have a time, usually at least once a day, and often while in the bath, when I use a more internalised line of connection to receive updates on anything fresh he may have said. His 'take' on things is usually interesting and thought-provoking as well as explanatory and reassuring, and I don't want to be left out!

This ability to speak to a Spirit Guide in what I can only call 'internal dialogue' develops naturally with practice, and I observe it happening with other friends and colleagues who have built up a volume of experience in having a Spirit Guide alongside them. It sometimes works on informal occasions when friends ask whether Gildas has any brief view of something. At other times I sense what I now know to be Gildas initiating a brief connection by making my left cheek itch. The comments he makes then are usually quite light or humorous asides. Once, at a large conference where we had to queue a long time for the 'help yourself' salad bar, one of the platform speakers said he felt that all our Guides and angels were joining in with what was a lovely, multi-dimensional, event. My left cheek itched, and Gildas said: 'Indeed we *are* but we are *not* queuing for salads.'

Practice and familiarity in this field will breed ease and delight, so do persevere.

Developing and strengthening your aura

Chapter 7 describes chakras and chakra connections and suggests ways of working with your chakras in order to strengthen your aura or subtle energy field for the work. If you want to progress with working with Spirit Guides, I must reiterate that it is essential to continue this work of aura strengthening.

In daily life, when we embark on an unfamiliar experience or routine, such as starting a different job, learning a new subject or trying out something we have never done before, we often feel that our energy levels are more quickly depleted than usual until we have built up familiarity with the task and/or greater stamina. Unless we are in training, we can't decide to go for a half-marathon run tomorrow or even next week. So it is with developing and strengthening our aura.

Exercise 11 on page 159 is an additional method of aura strengthening and also helps in psychic protection. Gildas has christened it 'the Russian doll exercise' because seven to eight bands of colour are built up, one inside the other, like the traditional Russian doll. Gildas's suggestion, as explained in Chapter 7, page 117, that we pay attention to keeping our etheric webs 'squeaky clean' is also pertinent for aura development and strengthening.

After years of practice I regularly sustain the connection with Gildas for about 45 minutes to enable him to give a lecture or 'face to face' guidance session. After a break, and probably some food (this work can make you hungry, and achieving altered states by fasting is not recommended), I can renew the contact again for about the same period of time; in a workshop group I will even sometimes renew the contact once more in the same day. The group helps in sustaining the energy required. In my private practice, however, I never do more than two one-to-one channelling sessions a day and rarely timetable one to follow immediately after the other. Usually, if we work significantly beyond the usual length of time for any reason, Gildas will 'look after' me by telling those who are perhaps persisting with questioning, that 'Ruth is coming to the end of the time for which she can maintain this level of communication'.

Although on the whole I find that working with Gildas tends to energise me, a particularly long session can make me feel a little ungrounded or 'otherworldly' for a while, and I need to sit still with my feet on the ground and practise the grounding exercise. Or I may practise grounding whilst taking my dog for a walk. A cup of tea with milk is also helpful for grounding when I have been in sustained channelling mode, I find.

As you progress, if you want to develop sustained channelling sessions you will find your own boundaries and limits, but extend them gently and never let others persuade you to go significantly beyond what you know is right and reliable for you. Channelling takes a great deal of mental concentration, and knowing your limits helps in keeping the communications that come through you clear and uncoloured.

What do my Guides expect of me now?

This is a question you may ask as you feel yourself ready to go beyond the scope of the exercises given in this book so far. The obvious answer is that we should put this question directly to our Spirit Guide, especially as we now have a more seriously developed contact. However, it might perhaps be a question that we are really asking not of our Guides but of ourselves: where do *I* want to go now? What do *I* want to develop now?

To have moved through all the exercises in this book to a place where you know that you can have serious contact with a Spirit Guide as, when and where you wish, means that you will have worked through a considerable amount of spiritual growth and self-knowledge. So the question as to whether you now want to put your gifts and abilities to a more outward and practical use, rather than keeping them as part of your inner development, can be a very serious one indeed.

Guides certainly do not *expect* anything of us; letting go of expectation of all kinds is a taxing but important step on the path of spiritual growth – Spirit Guides are well past this. There is a sense in which they may *hope* for, rather than *want* or *expect* certain things to develop from a serious connection with them. Many Spirit Guides are concerned to help us in these times, with healing, information, spiritual growth, teaching and the 'thinning of the veil' between the different other worlds and dimensions.

Your Guide may let you know that they have a certain area of interest, and this will often coincide with any special area of interest of your own. Healers, for example, often find that they develop a strong contact with a healing Guide, who will strengthen and focus their channelling of healing and support as well as their develop-ment of healing techniques, and may also pass on to them ways in which they can give further help to those who come to them for healing. Personal healing Guides may also encourage a healer to develop a wider and more professional healing practice.

Several people I know who have developed a firm connection to a Spirit Guide already have an interest in meditation and spiritual growth. They often seem to connect with a Guide who has similar interests (after all, which comes first, the chicken or the egg?). With a Guide firmly beside them, these people often go on to organise or lead meditation and spiritual growth groups. Their Guides may actively encourage them towards such leadership, but usually it is a development that evolves naturally.

Over all the years that I have been channelling, holding work-shops, healing and teaching, one or two people have felt the desire within themselves, as well as receiving encouragement from their Guides, to develop their channelling more profes-sionally. They have wished to teach others the art, to hold groups to support and hear channelled teachings, to run healing groups or training or to give specific guidance and channelled sessions for individuals.

If you want to put your channelling abilities out into the world, there are a number of ways in which you can do so, and your Guides will, usually, joyfully cooperate and bring the synchronicities and opportunities towards you that will allow or encourage your plans to manifest themselves. It is important, however, that you always recognise your own responsibility in making such decisions. Your Spirit Guide may well encourage you but should never drive you. Being over-driven by guidance can be a mark of serious colouring, as I discussed in Chapter 8, page 130. Even in my own story, where Gildas and I have an agreement that in this incarnation of mine we will develop cooperative work together, I nevertheless know that I am completely free to make a different choice at any time. I also know that I never will, because the work continues to develop and deepen, and being co-creative with Gildas is a life-fulfilling and delightful experience.

When we apply our channelling abilities to a more public or specific use with others, we help the Spirit Guides to extend the rainbow bridge of connection between their world and ours and to awaken human hearts and minds to the wider meanings and contexts of life. The Guides will relish the kind of contact that enables this to happen, but they will relish it and encourage it, not want or need it in the same way as human wants and needs.

Psychic protection

A book such as this would be incomplete without a mention of psychic protection. If you follow the advice consistently given here about training to reach the correct level of awareness so that you can meet your Spirit Guide and establish challenges and signals with him or her, as I discussed in Chapter 5, page 79), almost all the psychic protection you will need is built in. Working with your chakras, developing and strengthening your aura and pacing yourself in the first stages will all serve to ensure that you are making a safe connection between the dimensions. A strong, bright aura is not vulnerable to psychic attack. Chakras that are nourished and have a flow between them are also resistant to psychic attack or blockage. The grounded individual is resistant to psychic attack.

There are, however, fields of spiritual and psychic work, such as rescue circles, entity clearance and house or area clearing, where it is wise to know about more specific psychic shielding and protection.

These are specialist fields, and if you are drawn to them you need to find a reliable group or teacher who, as part of the experience, will also teach you the specific psychic protection appropriate to the work.

Where have I met my Spirit Guide before?

Almost everyone who feels the link to a Spirit Guide asks this question. Exercise 10 is a guided procedure that will help you know more about this. I do think such information can be of use in affirming the connection and bond between you and your Guide, but I have deliberately left addressing this until the end of this book because I don't think it should be specifically investigated too soon.

Of course, you may already have a definite idea about where you and your Spirit Guide have met before, because you may have sensed or seen your Guide in a particular role related to another lifetime. My very early senses of Gildas, when I was a child, were that he was an angel. I didn't know about Guides, but he is, like all Spirit Guides, a shining presence. Later, when he told me that he had been a white-robed monk in fourteenth-century France during his final life on earth, I realised that I had met him in that life as a young novice monk. I have performed exercise 10 a number of times, to pick up on previous connections with Gildas, although not specifically to concentrate on his French life. I have received a clear sense of a Native American life in which we met, and vague ones of Egypt and ancient China. This knowledge is interesting, and I feel it adds colour to the lines of connection between us, but it does not alter our working relationship now in any significant way.

So, if you want to know about past connections with your Spirit Guide, I hope the exercise will be helpful for you. What I most wish for you all, however, is a growing, loving, luminous, thread of unity with your Guide in the here and now, and a delight in all that this can add to your enjoyment of life.

Use these concluding exercises to give you a further range of possibilities for increasing your knowledge of, and friendship with, your Spirit Guide. The Russian doll exercise is included at this stage because it is a good way to revitalise your energy, strengthen your auric field and round anything off, so I have included it to complete this book.

Exercise 9: *Building a more informal meeting place with your Spirit Guide*

The following exercise helps you to use your inner landscape to find or build a meeting place that will offer you the opportunity for a more informal contact with your Spirit Guide than you have experienced at the rainbow bridge. Use it only when you feel you are familiar with your Spirit Guide and are therefore happy to invite him or her to come even more closely into your inner worlds. Follow the general preparation instructions given in Chapter 4, page 54 and exercise 1 on page 55.

1. Become aware of the rhythm of your breathing. Draw the breath into your heart centre or chakra, so that your heart chakra is activated and you travel on the heart breath into your inner landscape where you find yourself in your meadow.

2. Whilst in your meadow, take the opportunity to activate all your inner senses so that you see the colours and the objects, hear the sounds, smell the fragrances, touch the textures and taste the tastes.

3. Call your inner wise being or presence and your power animal to journey with you. Look out at your landscape and decide where would be a good direction in which to find or build an informal meeting place to meet your Spirit Guide when you want a more informal contact than when you go to the rainbow bridge. Ideally this should be at a place in your landscape that gives you a view over the surrounding

landscape but is not necessarily as high up as the plateau where your find the rainbow bridge.

4. Accompanied by your power animal and your inner wise presence, journey towards the place you have selected. It may be that on this journey you find a natural place that is bathed by sunlight, beside water or at a vantage point. Perhaps you will find a small, ready-built sanctuary or chalet, or a travellers' rest that is different from any you may also know at the rainbow bridge plateau. Perhaps you will find a suitable site on which to build a sanctuary, travellers' rest or chalet, to your own design. Perhaps you will find a house in which you know there is a library or special room where you could hold these more informal meetings with your Guide. It should be a place where you feel entirely comfortable and to which you will wish to return, not necessarily to embark on work with your Spirit Guide but simply to enjoy each other's presence and become more at peace with each other in an informal way.

5. If you are building your meeting place, you may need to return several times to complete the task, but once it is ready, just relax there and invite your Spirit Guide to join you and your power animal in this special place.

6. Rest and relax in each other's presence for up to ten minutes and then prepare to take your leave and return to your meadow.

7. Accompanied once more by your inner wise presence or being and your power animal, journey back to your meadow, knowing that you can return to this place in your landscape whenever you wish.

8. From your meadow, return to the breath in your heart centre and then to your everyday surroundings. Put a cloak of light with a hood right around you and be aware of your feet in contact with the ground.

9. Take time to keep a record of these journeys in your special book.

Exercise 10: *Where have I met my Guide before?*

This is a good exercise to do with a partner or even in a small group. You can also do it alone but in this case it is important to set an alarm to ring not more than 20 minutes from the start. Read the whole meditation through several times before you begin, and pay particular attention to the grounding instructions at the end.

1. Before you begin, take a piece of paper and write today's date – day, month and year – clearly on it. Put it where it will be easily visible and accessible at the end of this inner journey. Have coloured crayons near you and your special book on hand for any recording you may later wish to do. Follow the general preparation instructions given in Chapter 4, page 54 and set your alarm (this is particularly important if working alone).

2. Close your eyes and become aware of the rhythm of your breathing. 'Watch' your breath as it gradually slows down to a comfortable, natural tempo.

3. Ask your Spirit Guide to watch over you and to help you to see any past life information that might help with the growth of the bond between you in this present lifetime.

4. As you enter your inner being, find yourself walking in a

beautiful walled garden. The sun is shining warmly on the scene and the bricks of the walls are mellow.

5. Take time to explore every part of the garden – enjoying the plants and the way in which the garden has been laid out and carefully tended.

6. Curiously, you discover that there is a large mirror set in one of the garden walls. As you look into the mirror you realise that you are not looking at a here-and-now reflection, but are watching another scene from another time and seeing a lifetime in which you knew your Spirit Guide before, or to which your Spirit Guide wants you to acknowledge a link and connection.

7. As you continue to look into this mirror the story of this other life unfolds and you watch with interest. At any time that you do not wish to see any more, know that you can simply turn away from the mirror and walk through other parts of the garden, or that you can return through your heart breath to your outer, everyday, present world.

8. If you are happy to do so you can continue to look into the mirror until the alarm tells you that it is time to return.

9. See the images you have been watching in the mirror fade until all you are looking at is the reflection of your here-and-now self.

10. Turn from the mirror and walk through your favourite areas of the walled garden, feeling at peace. Sit for a while on a bench or seat, in the sunshine.

11. When it feels natural to do so, begin to come back to the

awareness of your body on the chair or floor, in your everyday surroundings. Connect with the normal rhythm of your breathing. Open your eyes and look around you. Place a cloak of light with a hood right around you. Get up and walk around the room, being particularly conscious of your feet on the floor.

12. Sit down again and take the piece of paper on which you wrote today's date and write that date again, in another colour.

13. Take your special book and make any notes or drawings you may wish to add to it.

Exercise 11: Developing and strengthening your aura (the Russian doll exercise)

This exercise helps to cleanse, strengthen and differentiate the layers of your aura. It is energising, healing and protective and helps to increase your stamina in maintaining contact with the rainbow bridge of communication between other worlds and dimensions. The layers are rather like a stacking Russian doll where one doll is placed inside another larger one, and then that is placed inside yet another larger doll until there are layers of dolls.

1. Eventually you can do this meditation in almost any position or situation, but first practise it standing, if possible, or sitting on an upright chair.

2. You will breathe seven bands of light and colour around your body from left to right, starting and ending at your feet, then seven more from the back of your body to the front, also starting and ending at your feet. When you visualise or imagine the colours, see them as vibrant and

translucent – like stained glass, when sunlight passes through it. The colours are: deep rose pink, amber, golden yellow, spring green, lapis lazuli blue, indigo and deep violet.

3. Stand easily and comfortably. Pay attention to the balance of your head on your neck. Place your feet comfortably apart, do not tense your shoulders or lock your knees. Relax any tension in the lower part of your body and rock your pelvis a little until you have a relaxed stance.

4. Before beginning the light and colour breaths, pay attention to your breathing. Imagine a breath, which starts underneath your feet on the in-breath and travels up the left side of your body to the crown of your head. Here you start the out-breath, which goes down the right side of your body to the starting position under your feet. Practise these breaths until the rhythm is flowing easily.

5. Now, begin the light and colour breaths. Visualising deep rose-pink light, breathe a band of this colour up your left side on the in-breath, keeping the colour band close to your physical body. At the crown of your head change to the out-breath and take the deep rose-pink colour down the right side of your body, letting it join under your feet.

6. Do the same with each colour in turn, moving slightly further out from your body as you breathe each new band, until you are surrounded with a rainbow of coloured light. Light and colour can interpenetrate with physical matter, so visualise the bands of light lying as evenly under your feet as they are around the rest of your body.

7. Once you have established the spectrum of light around you in this direction, continue to breathe evenly.

8. The next step is to breathe the light and colour bands around you from back to front. Again, you start under your feet, with deep rose pink; breathe it up the back of your body to the crown of your head, on the in-breath, and down the front of your body to join under your feet, on the out-breath. You end with violet, as before.

9. When you have breathed all the bands of light and colour from side to side and back to front, continue to breathe evenly and let each band of colour expand around and join around you until it forms an egg shape. Imagine a 'Russian doll' effect: you are in the centre, surrounded by seven layers of light and colour. Feel strengthened, energised, protected and secure.

10. Before you take up your normal tasks once more, visualise a silver layer of light enclosing the other seven. In this way, you take light and energy with you wherever you go, but are less vulnerable to any unwanted intrusion from the outer world.

11. When you know this exercise well, it is not always necessary to go through the complete breathing/visualisation – although it is a good meditative practice in itself. At any time when you feel vulnerable or in need of an energy boost, you can merely visualise the seven layers of light and colour surrounding you, with the final layer of silver as a container for the energy and to help you absorb all the healing which light and colour can bring.

Finally, I should like to share with you this favourite quotation of mine. It gives the only reason you may ever need for wanting to work with your Spirit Guide:

Ask not what the world wants, but what makes your heart sing, because what the world wants is people whose hearts sing.

SOURCE UNKNOWN

GLOSSARY

Akasha/ether is usually considered to be a fifth element in esoteric teaching. There is a progression from the tangible earth, water, fire and air, to the intangible akasha or ether. It is like a collective energy body for humanity, holding the imprint of everything each individual, group, family or race has ever known, done or is in the process of knowing and doing. It is also thought to have a relationship to the origins of sound and colour. Ether is not related to the chemical element but to the term 'the ethers', which is sometimes used to describe the other energetic planes and levels.

Akasha is also the element that is believed to hold an imprint which is the record of everything that we as individuals have ever known or lived in this lifetime or other lifetimes, as well as records of the entire collective experience of humanity. It is close to that which C. G. Jung described as 'the collective unconscious'.

Altered state (of consciousness) Electrical cycles in the brain can be measured and can vary according to what you are doing. There is a 'normal' range of cycles, known as the 'beta' rhythms, for everyday functions and the material world. When we sleep, we are mainly in 'theta' rhythm. Delta rhythms occur in the periods immediately preceding sleeping and waking. When during waking consciousness we are being particularly creative, 'alpha' rhythms may be present. Through meditation or hypnosis we may enter 'altered states' in which beta rhythms fade whilst alpha, delta and theta rhythms become more constant. In such states our physical bodies relax and we may have an expanded awareness in which the barriers of time and space are lessened.

Drugs may induce altered states but the cumulative side effects and other factors which often accompany drug-taking make them undesirable and usually counter-productive in any serious spiritual exploration.

Angels are direct reflections of Divine Consciousness. They are intermediaries and guardians helping the Divine plan to manifest itself on earth.

The elemental/devic/angelic hierarchy or life stream may be seen as moving from the Divine Consciousness towards earth, whilst the human stream of consciousness, which also includes discarnate Guides, may be seen as moving towards reunification with the Divine. The elemental/devic/angelic hierarchy is therefore separate from humanity. Discarnates are not angels, and angels will not take on human form or consciousness. Our guardian angels are different from our discarnate Guides and mentors. (See also **Guardian angels**.)

The elemental kingdoms include fairies, gnomes, elves and devas. Fairies traditionally look after plants, flowers and the earth. Books and cards depicting pictures of flower fairies are very popular. Other creatures look after the other elements: sylphs for air, undines for water and salamanders for fire.

Gnomes, goblins and elves are also associated with the element of earth, but they are often the tricksters of the elemental kingdoms who turn milk sour and play various other tricks on human beings who do not respect them and their presence.

Archetypes by dictionary definition are 'primordial images inherited by all'. Each human society is affected by forces such as peace, war, beauty, justice, wisdom, healing, birth, death, love and power. These are sometimes called 'the archetypes of higher qualities'. The essence of them defies definition and we use images, myths, symbols and personifications to help us in understanding their depth and breadth. Tarot cards, which have ancient origins, contain 22 person-ified or symbolised archetypes in the Major Arcana. These cover all aspects of human experience. They are: the Fool, the Magician, the High Priestess, the Empress, the Emperor, the Hierophant, the Lovers, the Chariot, Strength, the Hermit, the Wheel of Fortune, Justice, the Hanged Man, Death, Temperance, the Devil, the Tower, the Star, the Moon, the Sun, Judgement, and the World.

Chakras The word 'chakrum' is Sanskrit and means 'wheel'. Properly speaking, chakurm is the singular form and chakra the plural but in the West it is usual to speak of one chakra and many chakras. Much of the colour and energy of the auric field is supplied by the chakras. Clairvoyantly seen, they are wheels of light and colour interpenetrating with, affecting and affected by, the physical body. Chakras carry links to specific parts of the glandular system and might therefore be described as subtle glands. Most Eastern traditions describe a sevenfold major chakra system, at the same time acknowledging varying large numbers of minor chakras. The major chakras are: the crown (at the crown of the head); the brow (above and between the eyes); the throat (at the centre of the neck); the heart (in the centre of the body on the same level as the physical heart); the solar plexus (just under the ribcage); the sacral (two fingers below the navel); the root (in the perineum area). Working with the chakras aids physical, mental, emotional and spiritual health.

Daemons are not 'demons' but can be any personification of wise or guardian-like aspects of ourselves. People who may not believe in the other realms from which Guides come, but who nevertheless feel a connection with personified or animalised wisdom sources, may call these 'daemons'. *Chambers Dictionary* defines daemons as 'a spirit holding a middle place between gods and men', and 'daemonic' as 'supernatural; of power or intelligence more than humans; inspired'.

Discarnate can be a term used to describe anyone who has died, but in the esoteric field it is more often used to describe Spirit Guides and those who wish to communicate with us from the subtle planes that surround our material world of earth.

Extraterrestrials is the term used to describe any communicators who purport to be from stars or planets other than earth or the subtle planes that surround planet earth.

Guardian angels We each have a guardian angel who watches over us from before birth and accompanies our passage through death. Our guardian angel evolves from the elemental hierarchy to accompany us on our journey when our soul decides to take on another incarnation. When we die our guardian angel moves on to some other angelic task. (See also **Angels.**)

Higher self is part of the individual soul, as in soul and spirit. It is the growing consciousness of the soul that has an overview of all our lifetimes and decides on and reviews our tasks and purposes for each incarnation, ensuring that the soul gains all the experience necessary for full evolution. (See also **Soul and spirit.**)

House clearance/area clearance/entity clearance It is possible for some entities to live in an unclear state between this world and the next. This means that they inhabit the lower astral planes, which enables them to stay attached, in entity form, to places, people, houses and churches on the earth plane. They may cause depression or psychic phenomena, such as poltergeist activity around humans in incarnation. Some mediums or clairvoyants specialise in being able to talk to such entities in the places where they are causing disturbance and persuading them to move on. (See also **Lower entities.**)

Karma is an involved spiritual concept. In a nutshell, it is 'the law of cause and effect', and could be characterised by the biblical phrase: 'As ye sow so shall ye reap'. Karma dictates that every decision must have its fixed consequences, but that the decisions themselves are freely arrived at. Thus, the consequences of our past decisions condition our present lot.

Lower entities are unevolved beings or thought forms that exist on the lower levels of the astral plane. They sometimes 'haunt' places and buildings on earth as ghosts and are implicated in cases of humans being 'possessed' or 'obsessed' by unearthly entities. Such beings cannot impede the true guidance relationship with Spirit Guides if care is taken to train in maintaining a higher level of awareness in all attempts to make the guidance connection.

Psyche Analytic and transpersonal psychologists have shown how complex the human personality is. The psyche refers to the total being with all its drives, needs, conflicts, disease, health, gifts and potential.

Rescue circles In addition to lower entities and thought forms, some people who die may find it difficult to accept that they are dead and so tend to inhabit a twilight world between the planes of existence, unable to 'go into the light' and, though physically dead, still over-involved with the physical plane. This state may result from unresolved emotional issues at the time of death or sometimes as the result of violent or sudden death. Rescue circles are specialist groups who meet together to try to help such beings to accept that they are dead and to move on to the help and light and healing that is always awaiting them, but which they may be blocked from reaching because of a particular mental or emotional 'set' at the time of physical death. (See also **Lower entities** and **House clearance**.)

Shamanic/shamanism refers to a tradition and healing form that originated in Iceland and parts of Russia and also came to be practised by the North and South Native Americans. Shamans undergo rigorous training, which enables them to become seers and healers and to cross the boundaries between the planes. Neo-shamanism is a reawakening of the shamanic tradition.

Soul and spirit There are endless philosophic discussions about the differences between soul and spirit. Gildas (my discarnate guide) favours the distinction which sees the soul as yin and the spirit as yang. The soul is receptive, the spirit is active; the spirit incarnates while the soul oversees the incarnation and gathers experience, processing it for evolution. (See also **Yin and yang**.)

Soul group In Chapter 2 of this book a description is given of the soul and the process of many incarnations, using the analogy of an ear of wheat. The core of the ear is the soul and higher self, accumulating the knowledge and experience that is the basis of evolution; the grains on the ear are the personalities who have incarnated or who may yet incarnate; the life force in the stem is the spirit that animates each incarnation. Twin ears of wheat are twin souls, each having numerous aspects that have incarnated or have the potential to incarnate. Beyond this complexity of individual and twin souls we might say that the field of wheat is a soul group and other fields of wheat elsewhere would be other soul groups. Each soul group may have a shared evolutionary task or purpose that is ultimately for the benefit of the whole of the evolving human stream of consciousness.

Transpersonal therapy and counselling address the spiritual and behavioural needs and aspirations of human beings. They concentrate on the importance of finding a meaning in life and of being creative and fulfilled in living, relating and making choices.

Yin and yang are Chinese words for the basic but opposite aspects of creation. Yin is receptive, feminine and dark. Yang is active, masculine and light. In the traditional yin/yang symbol, one black and one white fishlike shape nestle together to form a perfect circle. The eye of the black shape is white and the eye of the white shape is black, showing that the seed of each is contained within the other.

FURTHER READING

Titles by Ruth White
Working with your Chakras, Piatkus, 1993
A Message of Love, Piatkus, 1994
Working with Guides and Angels, Piatkus, 1996
Chakras – A New Approach to Healing Your Life, Piatkus, 1998
Your Spiritual Journey, Piatkus, 1998
Karma and Reincarnation, Piatkus, 2000
Energy Healing for Beginners, Piatkus, 2002

Other titles

Roberto Assagioli, *The Act of Will*, Psychosynthesis and Education Trust, 2002
Maxwell Cade and Nina Coxhead, *The Awakened Mind: Biofeedback and the Development of Higher States of Consciousness*, Element, 1987
C. J. Cooper, *An Illustrated Dictionary of Traditional Symbols*, Thames and Hudson, 1979
James Hillman, *Re-visioning Psychology*, Harper and Rowe, 1975
Soozi Holbeche, *The Power of Gems and Crystals*, Piatkus, 1990
C. G. Jung, *The Archetypes and the Collective Unconscious*, Routledge, 1991
C. G. Jung, *Man and His Symbols*, Aldus Books, 1964
Abraham Maslow, *Toward a Psychology of Being*, Van Nortrand, 1962
Thomas Moore, *Care of the Soul*, Piatkus, 1992
Ken Wilber, *The Atman Project: A Transpersonal View of Human Development*, Quest Books, 1996

Index

Note: page numbers in *italics* refer to illustrations.